REAL JUSTICE

A POLICE
MR. BIG STING
GOES WRONG
• • •

THE STORY OF KYLE UNGER

RICHARD BRIGNALL

LORIMER

JAMES LORIMER & COMPANY LTD., PUBLISHERS
TORONTO

James Lorimer & Company Ltd., Publishers acknowledges the support of the Ontario Arts Council. We acknowledge the financial support of the Government of Canada through the Canada Book Fund for our publishing activities. We acknowledge the support of the Canada Council for the Arts which last year invested $24.3 million in writing and publishing throughout Canada. We acknowledge the Government of Ontario through the Ontario Media Development Corporation's Ontario Book Initiative.

ONTARIO ARTS COUNCIL
CONSEIL DES ARTS DE L'ONTARIO

Canada Council
for the Arts

Cover image: Winnipeg Sun

Library and Archives Canada Cataloguing in Publication

Brignall, Richard, author
    Real justice : a police Mr. Big sting goes wrong : the story of Kyle Unger / Richard Brignall.

For ages 13 and up.
Issued in print and electronic formats.
ISBN 978-1-4594-0863-0 (bound).--ISBN 978-1-4594-0862-3 (pbk.).--
ISBN 978-1-4594-0864-7 (epub)

    1. Unger, Kyle--Juvenile literature. 2. Undercover operations--Manitoba--Juvenile literature. 3. Confession (Law)--Manitoba--Juvenile literature. 4. Police questioning--Manitoba--Juvenile literature. 5. Homicide investigation--Manitoba--Juvenile literature. 6. Judicial error--Manitoba--Juvenile literature. I. Title.

HV8080.U5B75 2015   j363.2'32   C2014-907547-2
C2014-907548-0

James Lorimer & Company Ltd.,
Publishers
317 Adelaide Street West, Suite 1002
Toronto, ON, Canada
M5V 1P9
www.lorimer.ca

Distributed in the United States by:
Orca Book Publishers
P.O. Box 468
Custer, WA, USA
98240-0468

Printed and bound in Canada
Manufactured by Marquis in Montmagny, Quebec in February 2015.
Job #111642

*I WOULD LIKE TO DEDICATE THIS BOOK TO MY WIFE,
SHELLEY, AND MY PARENTS. WITHOUT THEIR FULL
SUPPORT, I WOULD NOT BE WHERE I AM TODAY —
FOLLOWING MY DREAM OF BEING A WRITER.*

CONTENTS

PROLOGUE

The past books I have written all involved a great sports team or an individual athlete. All overcame great obstacles to rise to the top of their sport. It is hard to question a final score of a game or what an athlete accomplished. The idea of reasonable doubt of the events is never brought up. They either won the game, accomplished the goal, or not.

I was then asked to write this book on Kyle Unger and his wrongful conviction. It became a learning experience. A young teenager in a small community in Manitoba had been sexually assaulted and brutally slain. People wanted to find a murderer and so did I. It was easy to point the finger at Kyle Unger. He was accused of the murder, convicted of the crime, and spent fourteen years in jail. When I first looked into the case, I thought Kyle Unger was guilty. I like to think I don't jump to conclusions, but I did with Kyle Unger. Emotion took over my decision-making ability.

I almost said no to writing this book, but I'm glad I didn't. I saw the real story emerge as I started to research the book. I saw how a justice system narrowed its focus on an individual and fit the evidence against him for the crime. In 1992, Kyle Unger was convicted of murder. A life was forever changed. That wrong was eventually made right. Unfortunately, the true murderer will never be convicted and punished for the crime.

This book will take the reader through the events around a murder, including the people involved, the investigation, and the trial. More importantly, the reader will see how the successful prosecution of Kyle Unger was eventually revealed to be a wrongful conviction. In 2009, he was acquitted of the crime.

Many people were affected negatively at every point during these events. But by the end of the story, it is possible for us to have a restored faith in Canada's justice system. During Kyle Unger's time in jail, the system evolved enough to right its previous wrongs against him. However, at the time of writing this book, there is an ongoing debate in Canada about the methods police forces use to gain confessions.

CHAPTER ONE

FESTIVAL WEEKEND

It was the beginning of another Manitoba summer. A time for people to get outside before another winter set in. A time when every weekend held a new activity or adventure. For teenagers in the southeast, the summer of 1990 started with the Woodstick Music Festival in June. It was a two-day event held at the Birch Run ski resort near the town of Roseisle, located 120 kilometres southwest of Winnipeg. Most of the teenagers from the surrounding area would attend.

Sixteen-year-old Brigitte Grenier couldn't wait to leave her parents' house in Miami. The Miami Collegiate grade 11 student was excited to attend her first concert. She wanted to hang out with friends, dance, and listen to music. She was a freckle-faced teenager with bright eyes and a pretty smile. People enjoyed her company and she was a popular student at school. They had just voted her to be the class president when school started back up in the fall. For now, she was heading up the graduation dance decorating committee. That celebration was scheduled for the week after Woodstick.

Brigitte was waiting for her best friend, Marlys Williment, to pick her up. They were going to the festival together, along with Marlys's boyfriend, Barry McTavish. Brigitte didn't have a boyfriend. But she knew there would be a lot of opportunities to meet boys at the festival. She had a personality that would easily attract them to her.

While Brigitte waited, her father joked about where she was going that night.

"Shouldn't it be called Wood*tick* Festival, instead of Woodstick?" teased Ron Grenier. He knew his youngest daughter didn't like wood ticks.

Brigitte stared at her father and then started to laugh.

"That's not funny, Dad."

Joking aside, Ron worried about his daughter going to the event. A lot of people were going to be there, and there would be drinking. And he had no way to protect her.

"Don't worry," said Brigitte. "I can take care of myself."

Soon after she'd said that, her ride pulled up to the house. Brigitte said goodbye to her dad and got into the waiting car. The three friends drove out into the night, excited about what might happen. To them, it was going to be a great evening.

2

CHAPTER TWO

THE LONERS

Attending the Woodstick Music Festival was a spur-of-the-moment decision for nineteen-year-old Kyle Unger and his best friend, John Beckett. It was something for them to do on a Saturday night. There wasn't always much going on in rural Manitoba. They lived in the middle of the prairie. It was a large, empty landscape of crop fields criss-crossed by dirt roads and secondary highways. There were no tall buildings or the bright lights and excitement of a city. Most teenagers dreamed of the day when they could leave.

Kyle and John were considered loners. They didn't have many friends in the communities surrounding the town of Carmen, mainly just each other for the past three years. Unger, who wasn't originally from this part of Manitoba, was tall and thin with a scruffy moustache. He found it hard to make new friends. So, he did everything with John.

Some of Kyle's problems making friends stemmed from his temper. He was kicked out of one school because of his unpredictable and violent behaviour. He had a reputation for being a troublemaker. Some people were afraid to be alone with him. All of this left a permanent mark on him. The shaggy, long-haired teenager was always an outsider.

On the night of June 23, 1990, they hitchhiked to the festival grounds. They looked like all the other teenagers in the crowd, wearing sneakers, jeans, and T-shirts. Their evening at Woodstick started around 8:30 p.m. Like most teenage boys attending the festival, they had a plan for the evening. It involved fun, getting drunk, and meeting girls.

There was a lot of room at the festival grounds. The main area was a large open field with the music stage at one end. People spread out over the rest of this area to sit, stand, and dance to the music being played on the stage.

The evening started with a game of football. Kyle and John joined in with a group of people they knew from school. For a short while, these loners were just two of the guys. When the game ended, they all sat and had beer together.

While they were playing football, Kyle had noticed Brigitte Grenier walk by. He'd always liked her at school.

He had gone to Miami Collegiate with her. She was one of only a few classmates who hadn't thought he was weird. He'd always considered her his friend.

After a few beers with the football players, Kyle and John went out to find Brigitte. They found her with some friends near the front of the festival stage. Kyle was excited to see her. He sat down next to her and they started to talk.

It was a good time to catch up since Kyle had quit school the previous year. He'd gotten a job in Alberta and had only recently returned home to visit. He talked to her about Alberta. She filled him in on what was happening at school. John sat there, silent.

After twenty minutes of conversation, Kyle and John left to see what was happening around the festival. They eventually joined back up with the football crowd. Everybody was drinking heavily. Many were drunk, including Kyle and John.

The alcohol was having a bad effect on Kyle's behaviour. At one point, he threw fellow football player Chris Fehr to the ground. They rolled around like they were play fighting. Chris grew tired of Kyle. He held him down on the ground for a while. Once Kyle settled down, Chris got up and told Kyle to "buzz off!"

Seeing that they were not welcome anymore, Kyle

and John roamed the festival grounds. Close to a thousand people had shown up. The two friends weaved their way through the crowd. It was so densely packed, they lost each other a couple of times. They eventually wanted to take a break and left the crowd together. They sat down on the ground, talked, and watched what was going on at the festival.

At one point, after leaving the crowd, Kyle disappeared for ten minutes. When he came back to John, he showed him a little square piece of paper on his tongue. It was a hit of acid, LSD.

The last band of the night was called Tooth and Nail. Kyle saw this as his last chance to dance with Brigitte. Since he liked her, he thought maybe she would like him, too. The two teens went on another search for Brigitte.

She wasn't at the spot where she had been sitting before, near the bandstand. But her stuff was still there, so they thought she might come back. They sat down to wait for her. The music continued and Brigitte didn't show up, so they soon found some other girls to dance with.

Then Kyle noticed Brigitte. She was dancing with another guy. He didn't know who this guy was. They were dancing close. Kissing each other. Touching each other. He didn't think it was normal for her to do that type of dancing.

Kyle was a little jealous seeing her dancing with another guy. He wanted to be that guy. The only way he could be with her was to break them up. He went up to Brigitte and tried to gain her attention. "You are a hard person to find," he joked.

Brigitte brushed him off. She wasn't interested in him at that moment. The look she gave Kyle told him to get lost. The two guys left Brigitte so she could continue dancing with her new friend.

Along with dancing in front of the bandstand, the other popular thing to do was hang out at the large bonfire. Kyle and John found their way there. At one point, Kyle went into the bush surrounding the festival site to go to the washroom. He came back with some interesting news.

He tapped John on the shoulder. "Guess who I seen in the bush? Brigitte, going at it with some guy."

The band was still playing. John fell asleep. Kyle wanted to have his own experience with a girl. He left the bonfire to meet a girl. Any girl.

About a half-hour later, Kyle woke John up. He told him he had gotten what he went looking for. John knew his best friend well. He was used to him lying about what he did. He didn't believe Kyle's story about having sex.

Once the music stopped, people began leaving the festival stage area. Some left for home, while others went to their campsites on the festival grounds. Kyle and John continued to hang around the bonfire. It gave them a chance to sober up from drinking. And time for Kyle to continue to tell stories people didn't believe.

By 4:30 on Sunday morning, the two friends were ready to leave. They hitched a ride from the festival grounds and arrived at John's house by 5:00 a.m. Kyle slept there for a while. He eventually got up and started to walk home. On the way, his mother picked him up and took him home to Roseisle.

3

CHAPTER THREE

YOUNG LOVE

Brigitte spent most of the night at Woodstick with her best friend, Marlys Williment. People were drinking all over the place. There didn't seem to be anyone policing it. It was part of the festival experience. Brigitte was drinking, too, and hanging out with friends.

One of the people she met at the festival was Kyle Unger. Marlys didn't like him; most people didn't. But Brigitte was seen as a person who was able to show sensitivity to everyone she dealt with. She had always had a soft spot for Kyle. She knew he had a hard time fitting in. That was why she tried to be his friend.

They talked at the beginning of the evening, by the bandstand. But by the end of the night, she was more interested in Tim Houlahan, a guy she had just met. Another friend, Steven Armstrong, introduced her to him. Tim was a Carmen Collegiate student. Carmen was close to Miami. He was seventeen years old and still had one year of high school left. People said he was someone who could always make you laugh. The type of guy people thought was fun to be around. But he was also known to get moody when he drank.

It must have been a good match because Brigitte and Tim were quickly seen on the dance floor. They danced close to each other. They kissed and touched each other. Things between them quickly progressed.

They were still dancing close when Marlys was leaving with her boyfriend. It was around 1:30 Sunday morning. Brigitte was supposed to go home with them, but she didn't want to go yet. She wanted to stay and dance with Tim.

Marlys was worried things might get out of hand. She didn't want Tim to take advantage of her. Brigitte told her not to worry. They were not going to have sex.

"Don't worry, Marlys. I'll still be a virgin tomorrow," Brigitte said to her best friend.

Brigitte got her knapsack from where they were sitting by the stage, and Marlys's boyfriend gave her his Nike sweatshirt to keep warm. She told them she would find a ride home with somebody at the end of the night. Then Marlys and Barry left Brigitte behind with Tim.

Once they were left alone, Brigitte and Tim left the dance floor. The music was loud and they wanted to go to a quieter place. They made their way to a nearby wooded and secluded part of the resort . . .

No one saw Tim again until around 4:00 a.m. He wasn't with Brigitte. He sat down with his friends around the bonfire. He looked very dirty. His clothing was muddy. His face was dirty and scratched. Blood was clearly visible on his chin.

At first, Tim was quiet. People left him alone for a while because he didn't look like he was in great shape. But his physical appearance eventually made them curious.

"Hey, man, what happened to you?" asked one friend.

Tim sat there quietly, not showing if he heard his friend or not.

"I would hate to see the other guy," joked that same friend, trying to lighten up the mood.

The bonfire burned bright in the centre of the crowd. They all sat, relaxed, except for Tim. His silence created a tension and made things awkward among them. He eventually started to tell his story.

"I was with a girl in the bush," said Tim. Some of his friends did their best to hold back their laughter.

"That's one tough girl," joked another friend.

"Actually, she was quite nice," said Tim. "After I was with her, I was jumped by a guy in the bush. It came as a surprise. He beat me up pretty good."

"Are you sure it wasn't her father getting back at you?" yelled out one friend.

Everyone started to laugh and continued to joke around with each other. Once Tim had told them his story, he lightened up. He started to talk more and joke around. He had more beer before he left the bonfire.

When they were leaving the area early Sunday morning, Tim and a friend stopped at the entrance to the festival. They set fire to the contents of a barrel. When they got to his friend's home, Tim ate a hot dog and went to bed.

4

CHAPTER FOUR

GRISLY FIND

John Graham and Fraser Kulba were biking around Birch Run ski resort. It was a beautiful Sunday morning, June 24, 1990. They enjoyed biking through the wooded areas of the resort.

At around 10:00 a.m., the two bikers stopped near a creek. Something in the creek caught their eye. They were hoping it wasn't what they thought it was.

"There's a body in the creek!" Fraser cried out in horror.

At first, John didn't believe him. He thought it might have been a department store mannequin. He picked up a stick, walked to the edge of the creek, and touched it to see if it was real. Instantly, he knew it was a woman. They were both in shock by the dead body in front of them. Not many people have seen a corpse.

"What should we do now?" questioned Fraser,

looking around to see if anybody was there. He wished he could tell somebody.

"I guess we should find someone to call the police," said John.

"I'll go," replied Fraser. "You stay to make sure nobody disturbs the body."

Fraser ran from the creek and up a hill. He followed a trail through the bush. It led to the open field where the Woodstick Festival had taken place. As he ran, he yelled for help. Nobody was around to help him.

He eventually found a festival worker, who found the property owner. They called the police after seeing the body for themselves. John continued to stay near the body. It was hard, even scary, for him, being that close to a dead body. He did it because it was the right thing to do.

Constable Ron Muir from the RCMP detachment at Carmen took the call. It was the type of call rural cops expected would happen only in the city. Somebody had found a body in a creek. His quiet Sunday morning was shattered.

Constable Muir arrived at the resort and set up police tape to protect the scene. Other RCMP officers, media, and the general public would eventually come to the murder scene, so it was important no evidence was disturbed. The police would need it to catch the killer.

They started their investigation in a big area. The body was found in a creek behind the main festival stage. The main stage was at one end of a large open field. Behind that stage was a dark opening in the trees. That was the start of the small trail that led down to the creek where the body was found. Along the left edge of that trail was an area with very long grass. Some of that grass was all broken down, flat on the ground. The police would find a lot of the evidence there.

The police divided the grassy area into a grid of smaller areas. Then they searched each section of the grid on their hands and knees. They were looking for clues. Along with the body, evidence helps to create the story of the murder. Once the police have gathered evidence, they try to piece together what may have happened and use this information to find the murderer.

The investigators found physical evidence across the search area. They found muddy, blood-soaked jeans with the legs ripped in two, torn women's underwear, bloodied socks, as well as a T-shirt and a Nike sweatshirt. A lot of the evidence looked as if it had been torn right off the body of the victim. Even her shoes were tossed in different directions.

Along with pieces of clothing, police found blood and hair evidence. But the most important piece of evidence

at this time was a knapsack. It contained enough information, including a high school photo of Brigitte, to
tell investigators this was probably the body of Brigitte
Grenier.

Three feet from the edge of the creek was a bare,
muddy area. Brigitte's body was in the water, two to three
feet away from the muddy shore. There were footprints in
the mud. Whoever dumped the body would have had to
walk a few feet through the mud and would have gotten
very muddy shoes. Brigitte's head and the right side of
her body were under the muddy creek water. Blood ran
down her thigh. On Sunday afternoon at 5:25 p.m., her
body was removed from the water. She was completely
covered with muck and mud. It was a gruesome sight for
everybody at the scene.

The medical examiner quickly found that she had
suffered terribly before she died. There was extensive
bruising across her eyes and the bridge of her nose, and
her lips were swollen. She looked like she had been beaten
in the face. Red marks on her throat indicated she had
been strangled. Her body had been violated with long,
sharp sticks. There were also bite marks on the victim's
breasts and one arm.

★ ★ ★

Ron Grenier's next meeting with his daughter was an experience he didn't wish upon anyone. The RCMP were not quite sure if the corpse belonged to Brigitte or to her sister because the body was found with two sets of identification. Police reluctantly called Ron to identify the body when his brother Emile (Brigitte's uncle) couldn't make the ID. The body was too badly beaten.

"I didn't even recognize her," Emile told reporters gathered outside the Carmen RCMP detachment. "When you can't even identify your own niece, it's pretty bad." He pleaded with people to come forward with information about the murder.

"Every murder is brutal, but this one was particularly bad," RCMP spokesperson Constable Wyman Sangster said. By this time, a massive police investigation was underway. "This is one of the most horrifying murders we've experienced in the history of the RCMP in this province. We're not ruling out anything. We're fairly confident that a person who attended the event was responsible for the murder."

A teenage girl was dead. A murderer was alive and could be living in this small rural community.

CHAPTER FIVE

TO CATCH A KILLER

The Brigitte Grenier murder investigation was too big for the small-town RCMP detachment in Carmen. When the body was discovered, they called Winnipeg for help. Kathleen King, from the RCMP General Investigation section in Winnipeg, travelled to Carmen that day. On arrival, she took charge of the investigation.

As officers gathered physical evidence, King took statements from civilian witnesses. Just like evidence, statements help create a story.

"My first thought was — where do you start?" said Constable King. "You start at the body and move out."

King began gathering statements from people who knew Brigitte. Marlys Williment, Brigitte's best friend, was the last known person to see Brigitte alive. Marlys gave an account of what had happened during the evening at the festival. She told King who Brigitte had talked to. The list included John Beckett, Kyle Unger, and Tim Houlahan.

King talked with John and then went to find Kyle. It was Sunday afternoon and he was camping in Stephenfield Park, thirteen kilometres west of Carmen. At the campsite, King and another RCMP constable got out of the vehicle and approached Unger. He was wearing the same clothes he'd had on at the festival. The clothing, like many teenagers' attire, appeared to be well worn, but not dirty at all. His shoes also appeared to be clean.

He asked the police if this was about the death. He stated that he had heard that a girl had drowned. He'd heard they found the body of Brigitte Grenier. He said she was a close friend.

Kyle was taken to the police squad car. At this stage, Kyle was being questioned as a witness, not as a suspect. He had seen Brigitte at various points during the night. He sat in the car and gave his statement about what he did and what he saw at the festival. He mentioned how Tim Houlahan was dancing closely with Brigitte. When asked for a hair sample, Kyle was quick to reply. "Sure, if you want some of my hair, I've got lots," he said.

After the interview, the two RCMP officers noted how Unger was very co-operative. He wasn't nervous to talk with them. He was not believed to be a suspect. To them, he didn't fit the story of a man who had just killed Brigitte Grenier.

Tim Houlahan was next on King's interview list. He was asked to come down to the Carmen RCMP detachment. He arrived on Monday, June 25, at 6:00 p.m. He had visible marks on his face and hands. He also had bruising around his eyes that indicated he had been in a fight or had been assaulted. He was visibly nervous.

The police learned that Tim was seventeen years old. At that age, he was protected under the *Young Offenders Act*. This meant he needed his parents present to make a statement to police. He was allowed to leave to play baseball while the police contacted his parents.

Before Tim left, the police made some casual comments they should not have. They told him that, from the beginning, they believed two people were involved in the murder. At this point, they were thinking Tim played a part in the murder. After he was told there was a room full of evidence, Tim looked like he would cry.

At 11:20 p.m., Tim returned to the detachment with his lawyer, Ms. Brenda Keyser. He did not have to give a signed statement to the police yet because his parents were still not present. Based on his injuries, though, the police made him their prime suspect.

On Tuesday, June 26, the police went to Tim Houlahan's residence. They had a search warrant to look for evidence linking Tim to the murder. Pieces of Houlahan's clothing were seized from his home. They found a muddy pair of jeans in a cardboard box. In the basement, they found a muddy T-shirt.

Tim was arrested based on the evidence found at his home and the statements of witnesses at the festival. He was placed in a detention cell at the Carmen jail. Police did not reveal to the public that they had a suspect in custody. Even if they had, they wouldn't have been able to say his name because he was protected under the *Young Offenders Act*. Anybody under the age of eighteen arrested or involved in a crime cannot have their identity revealed.

On Wednesday, June 27, Tim gave the police his statement in the presence of his parents and his lawyer, Ms. Keyser. Tim had been given a significant amount of time to consult with his counsel, and based on what the police had told him earlier, he had come up with a story to fit their theory of two people involved with the murder.

"I attended the festival with friends," said Tim, as he started to give the police his statement. "I was introduced to Brigitte. After dancing together, we went into the woods and had sex. It was consensual sex.

"After we were done, we both wanted to go to the bonfire. That's where my friends were. As we walked through the woods, she wanted to pee. She asked me to wait for her. After fifteen to twenty minutes, I didn't see any sign of her. I went to the festival washrooms, but they were empty. Then I started to look around for her in the wooded area. I called out her name. She never answered."

The room was silent as Tim gave his statement to the police. The murder investigation was four days old. They were relieved to have a suspect.

Tim continued. "I started to walk down another path and called out her name. I saw a trampled-down area of grass and mud and stuff. I went there, thinking she might be there. I then slipped and fell down. I got up. When I bent down to pick up my hat, I noticed a stream of light coming through the trees. It was then that I noticed the dark patch of blackened reddish stuff. It didn't look like mud or anything. I thought it was blood. I looked around again, and I was listening to see if I could hear anything. I didn't hear anything. I didn't see anything.

"I got scared and took off. I took off running and ended up over on the far side of the stage. I stopped there and sat down. I was catching my wind, and I was wondering what I'd seen and thinking about it, and somebody came up from behind and said something to me. Not sure what he said.

"I started to rise, turned my head, but I didn't get all the way to look," continued Tim. "I didn't get a good look at him. And then he shoved me and then I got almost up again after he shoved me and then I got hit. That's the last thing I remember, is that I got hit the first time. And then after that, I don't remember anything."

Tim finished his statement by telling the police he woke up, went to the bonfire, and then left. Tim did his best to describe the man who assaulted him. He said he remembered him having a moustache and shoulder-length hair. He said the man who assaulted him was six feet tall, wide shouldered, and had a deep, acid-type voice.

Once Tim gave his statement, the police made him plot his movements that night. Then Constable King asked a few more questions.

"Do you know an individual named Kyle Unger?" asked King.

"Ah, yes, I do," replied Tim.

"Did you see him that night?"

"No."

"Do you know John Beckett?"

"Yes."

"Did you see him?"

"No."

"What type of individuals are they, like from school?"

"They're not the greatest students and kind of a little wild and stuff," answered Tim.

Police asked Tim if the man who punched him was Kyle Unger. Tim said it wasn't Unger. Tim made sure his first statement gave the police a perfect explanation of why his clothing was covered in mud and blood. The police interest in Unger gave Tim an idea. If he could place Kyle Unger at the scene of the crime, he could make the police think that Unger was the person who killed Brigitte.

After giving his statement, Tim was released from police custody to his lawyer and parents. Without knowing it, Kyle Unger had gone from being a witness to a prime suspect. Tim's description of his assailant was detailed enough for the RCMP to conclude that he was identifying Kyle Unger. This happened even though Tim said the assailant wasn't him.

6

CHAPTER SIX

POINTING FINGERS

Brigitte Grenier's slaying left the region in shock. They were towns of trusting people. Miami Collegiate cancelled its first Safe Grad dance. People were afraid to go out at night. They were frightened because a murderer was still on the loose, and it might be someone they knew.

When the investigation first began RCMP constable Sangster issued a public appeal for information. An estimated four hundred people had been camping within five-hundred metres of where police believed Brigitte had been killed.

"We've got some leads, but we're hoping there's still someone out there we haven't talked to who might have some information we need," Sangster said in his appeal.

The community tried its best to help out the police. But after an initially valuable outpouring of information regarding the murder, the community threatened to become a liability. The police were expressing concern over unproven accusations and rumours being spread in nearby rural communities. The community was conducting its own investigation. People had their own theories. It got out of hand.

Sangster said that by Tuesday, June 26, they had identified and contacted a suspect in the slaying of Grenier.

"Some information came to light Monday night and yesterday morning that has resulted in us identifying a suspect," Sangster said on Wednesday, July 27. "We have narrowed the focus of this investigation. He's been contacted, but I can't say any more at this time."

Some reports made it sound as if the police were close to laying charges in the case, but were allowing a murderer to move freely in the community. Sangster said that was not the case.

After Tim was released into his parents' custody, the police continued to mount evidence against him. Blood on Tim's shoe came from Brigitte. Scalp hair on Brigitte's pants matched Tim's. A pubic hair on her sock also matched Tim's. The RCMP built a strong case against Tim. It was strong enough to allow them to arrest him on Friday, June 29. He was officially charged with the first-degree murder of Brigitte Grenier.

When in custody, he was asked to give an impression of his teeth. Brigitte had bite marks on her body. They wanted to see if Tim's impression matched those marks. Tim refused to give this to the police. Instead, Tim gave a second, more revealing statement to the police. He gave them exactly what they wanted to hear.

"Right after having sex, somebody came up and punched Brigitte," Tim said to the RCMP in his second statement. "I didn't recognize him at first and I asked him what he thought he was doing. He then turned to me, pushed me down, and then kicked me. I recognized it was Kyle Unger. He grabbed Brigitte. He was fighting with her and fought her down to the bottom of the hill, where that matted area was. I followed to see if I could help her or see what he was doing.

"Kyle said to her, 'So, you don't like me,' and then he started to choke her. I pushed him off her. Then he got up, pushed me down, and started kicking and punching me. And then told me to shut up and stay out of it. He started choking her again. He ripped her clothes off. Continued to strangle her and hit her in the face. I yelled a couple of times, but he told me to shut up or else something might happen.

"He just kept going and going and going, hitting her, and hitting her, and hitting her, and then he'd stop. Then he picked up a stick and started hitting her over the head, the face, and the body. She wasn't moving at this time and she hadn't been moving since he first dragged her down there and started choking her. After that, I never saw her move again.

"I got up, tried to run away, but tripped. I fell and he put the boots to me and dragged me back. He told me to settle down or else. He ordered me to come over and punch her a couple of times. I was afraid of him after what I'd seen he had already done to her. I was afraid of what he'd do to me. I went down and hit her twice. I backed away and he went back to punching her and kicking her.

"He ordered me to come over and help him. I went and he told me to help him carry her down to the water and then carry or drag her in. We ended up going down there and we put the body in the river. He told me not to say anything or else he'd come and find me and then he'd beat me up. Then a little while later, I woke up. I was somewhere else, I was woke up, and I had mud and blood on me. I went out to the bonfire and that's where everybody was."

The police had the information they wanted. They had a second person involved in the murder. They had their second suspect, Kyle Unger, as the murderer.

Tim made a statement that helped his case. He wanted to be found innocent of the crime. His statement showed him as a victim and Kyle Unger as the killer.

But, the police were still suspicious of Tim. After his new statement, they asked him a few questions.

"Why didn't you tell the police that night?"

"Because I was afraid," answered Tim. "I didn't want to finger Kyle then, and also, I was afraid I would get into trouble with the police because of, like, my shoes and mud and stuff all over my clothing and everything. I felt scared and terrified."

The RCMP's focus turned to Kyle Unger.

7

CHAPTER SEVEN

PRIME SUSPECT

At the festival, Kyle Unger had told his friend John that he liked Brigitte Grenier. He said that he wouldn't have minded asking her out on a date. Four days later, on Wednesday, June 27, they were both outside the church, waiting for her funeral to begin. They stood together and looked toward the cemetery beside the church. They wondered where she was going to be buried. Then they saw a mound of dirt.

Kyle joked around to cut the tension of the moment. He pretended to be nervous and said he thought the police suspected him. He didn't know how right he was. They would use every move he made to gauge his innocence or guilt.

On the same day as the funeral, the two friends visited the festival grounds. Kyle wanted some police tape from the murder scene to put across his bedroom door.

John was uncomfortable about being there. They drove around the resort, but didn't know where the body was found. They swept through the entire festival grounds, looking for the crime scene. They eventually found the place, recognizing it from television reports.

John did not want to leave the truck. Kyle got out and looked around. He noticed an area where the police had made foot moulds. That made him realize how stupid it was to be walking around the site. His footprints were there now. He returned to the truck to tell John about how his footprints could make him a suspect. They then drove away and left the area.

★ ★ ★

The police interviewed Kyle only once during their initial investigation. They talked with John five times. They searched his home for evidence. Their questions focused on Kyle. John had no direct knowledge as to whether Kyle was responsible for what happened. He said Kyle exaggerated his stories.

At first, Kyle had shown no concern about being a possible suspect. The two friends talked to each other about their interviews with the police. The whole investigation was interesting to them. Kyle eventually asked John if he had said anything that would get him in trouble. He was starting to think he was a suspect in Brigitte's murder.

Kyle's suspicions were not far from the truth. He shouldn't have worried about John, though. It was Tim Houlahan's second statement to police on Friday, June 29, that made him the prime suspect. It had been what the police were waiting to hear. Tim had been arrested the day he made that second statement and charged with first-degree murder. After his statement, police made the call to arrest Kyle Unger on the same charges.

On that day, RCMP constable Roger Tournier was on patrol in Carmen. He saw Kyle walking down Main Street. A different RCMP constable stopped Kyle and officially arrested him. After giving him his Charter rights, Kyle was taken to the Carmen RCMP detachment. He was charged with the first-degree murder of Brigitte Grenier. Kyle was very calm. He was searched and allowed to telephone a lawyer. Constable King then interviewed him.

Kyle was very co-operative. He agreed to give dental impressions. He gave blood and hair samples. He most readily supplied everything. He even thanked the constables for the way they treated him. After he was arrested, the police searched his parents' house and property. In

Kyle's bedroom, they found a photograph of Brigitte. A newspaper clipping from June 28 about the murder was taken from the glove box of his truck.

Kyle Unger's life was about to change. He went from witness, to suspect, to being charged with first-degree murder. Life would never be the same. He wouldn't be that young man with a harmless crush on a girl. He was now the person accused of murdering an innocent teenager.

8

CHAPTER EIGHT

PUBLIC ENEMY

The evening of Friday, June 29, was warm and breezy. Tim and Kyle were inside the Carmen RCMP detachment, being processed. Outside the detachment, news reporters and members of the public mingled with the investigating officers. The RCMP were preparing to make the announcement about the arrests.

Watching the people gathering for the news conference was Kyle's father, Wayne. He sat quietly in the parking lot in a blue pickup truck. Also attending were six of Brigitte Grenier's Miami Collegiate classmates and several members of her family.

Constable Sangster eventually announced that they had arrested two suspects. He said they arrested Kyle Wayne Unger, nineteen years old, and an un-nameable seventeen-year-old.

"When the charges were laid, there was no joy. Just

relief," said Constable Sangster. He noted that there were always two suspects in the case. "The two accused were identified as suspects almost immediately."

Sangster continued with his statement to say that the officers made no secret of the fact that they were relieved. The veteran police who attended the scene of the crime were overwhelmed with emotion as they retraced the events that led to Brigitte's death. Forty officers were involved in the investigation. Some had worked up to twenty hours per day. They announced the arrest, but could not release all the information about the case.

"Our reaction is relief," said Gerald Grenier, Brigitte's uncle. "I think the entire community is relieved."

The communities of Miami, Carmen, and Roseisle were small and close together, perhaps too much so — the families of the victim and suspects in this case lived less than twelve kilometres away from each other. Almost everyone knew each other by name or face. "We were all hoping it wouldn't be someone local," said Gerald Grenier. "But it was, and that will be hard."

The only person named during the arrest announcement was Kyle Unger, because Tim Houlahan's identity was protected under the *Young Offenders Act*. The entire focus of Brigitte's murder was on Kyle. He became the most hated person in Manitoba.

"I have never met the suspect's parents. But if I ever do, I don't know if I can be nice to them, even though I know it's not their fault," said Brenda Lehmann, owner of Lehmann's Restaurant in Miami. Just remembering that Kyle came to her restaurant disgusted her. "It's going to be a very long time before people forget."

9

CHAPTER NINE

FREE MAN

Trials can be expensive, especially a double first-degree murder trial. The court wanted to make sure the Crown had a solid case against the accused. Witnesses and evidence were brought forward in the preliminary hearing. The Crown had to show they had a strong enough case to go to trial. Kyle's lawyer, Hersh Wolch, wanted the opposite. He argued the Crown didn't have enough of a case against his client.

Kyle spent nearly five months in the Winnipeg Remand Centre before the hearing. He was locked away from family and friends. People in his community believed he was the killer. Students from Miami Collegiate went to the hearing. They gave Kyle dirty looks throughout the proceedings. But being charged is not the same as being guilty. These people still clung to the belief that someone arrested must be guilty.

At the same time that Kyle was locked up, Tim was a free man. He was awarded bail after being arrested because he was a young offender. He was released and returned home. Nobody in the community knew he was the co-accused in the murder trial. He got to live like it never happened. He was still protected by the *Young Offenders Act*.

Eventually people in this area figured out Tim was the un-named minor arrested for Brigitte's murder. Some parents wanted him removed from Carmen Collegiate. School board members did not respond adequately to parents' concerns about Tim's presence in school. Parents threatened to pull their children from school. Some followed through with this threat. Eventually, Tim was ordered by the school board to continue his studies at home.

The preliminary hearing lasted over four days. The Crown used Tim's second statement as the backbone of their case against Kyle. Wolch showed how witnesses at the festival were with Kyle all night. The witnesses said he didn't look different at the end of the night, or have any dirt or mud on him. The bite marks on Brigitte did not match Kyle. A hair found on Brigitte's sweatshirt might be a match to Kyle, but Wolch argued that it could have come from when they talked earlier in the night.

It all came down to a final decision on December 11, 1990. Crown Attorney Bob Gosman told provincial judge Charles Rubin that after a careful review of the evidence, the justice department had decided to enter a stay of proceedings. They didn't think there was enough evidence against Kyle to proceed to trial. There would still be a first-degree murder trial against Tim. He was formerly unknown to people, but by this time, he had been elevated to adult court from youth court. But his name would not be released until the beginning of his trial.

Kyle was a free man, almost. The RCMP would continue to investigate the case. New charges could be laid against him if their investigation turned up anything linking him to the murder. The charge could be reinstated at any time within the following twelve months. The RCMP thought they had enough evidence to charge Kyle. The justice system thought different.

Kyle walked out of the Manitoba Law Court building around 11 a.m. on December 11, 1990. The media swarmed him. He expressed that he wanted to put it all behind him as fast as possible. He feared that people would shun him. He knew small-town life. People would refuse to believe his innocence.

"I guess I'm nervous about some of my old friends," said Kyle. "I knew I was innocent, my family knew I was innocent." He said he wasn't angry over what happened. He knew the evidence couldn't prove he had a hand in the killing.

Treva Unger, Kyle's mom, looked more relieved than happy after hearing the stay of charges. "I'm just in shock, but I believed it was going to work out," said Treva. "I believed he was innocent right from the start. A mother knows." Treva, a warm, dark-haired woman, admitted her son might have a difficult time resuming his life. There were strong feelings against him in their rural community. "He's just got to try to put his life together, one day at a time," she said.

Residents of these tiny rural communities couldn't believe the charges against Kyle were stayed. They didn't believe in his innocence. If he returned, it would be to a hostile community where many residents long ago considered him guilty.

"They're releasing him into a dangerous situation," said Miami resident Dennis Lehmann. "The man cannot walk the streets right now. We've hated this man's guts for a few months now."

Kyle didn't realize how much his life was damaged. Public opinion was against him. He couldn't return to live with his parents. Finding a job was difficult. For the previous five months, he had been Manitoba's biggest monster.

He eventually got the second chance he needed. While visiting the Portage La Prairie mall, he saw a booth that interested him. The Hickory Hollow Hobby Farm was looking for workers. Marilyn Atkey was the owner of the farm located outside Austin, Manitoba.

Kyle travelled to the farm and asked Marilyn for a job. He told her he had been charged with murder but that he was innocent. Marilyn didn't doubt the story. Kyle said he felt the charges had ruined his life and that people would never accept him. Marilyn took a chance on Kyle and hired him. He was hired to look after the animals, do odd jobs, and give horse rides. He worked for room and board, and a modest salary. It seemed Kyle's life was back on track.

10

CHAPTER TEN

KYLE'S NEW FRIENDS

On June 13, 1991, nearly a year after Brigitte's murder, a motor home broke down outside the Hickory Hollow Hobby Farm. It had a New Brunswick licence plate. Kyle, now twenty years old, came over to see if anyone needed help. A man named Larry opened the door. He had a few days of stubbly beard growth and was wearing scruffy clothes, a ball cap, and had an earring. There was another person in the camper, named Greg.

"You got any hoot?" Kyle asked after introducing himself. He hoped to score some dope from the men. To Kyle, they looked like people who would have drugs. Larry told Kyle drugs were not their scene. He said they were passing through on their way to the Calgary Stampede. They hoped to find work there.

Kyle took a liking to the two men. Marilyn let them stay overnight. They offered to work around the farm to pay for their stay while parts were being ordered for repairs. When Kyle wasn't working, he would talk with them. "I just got outta jail, a half-year ago for murder," said Kyle to his new friends one night. "I spent six months in jail for it. I was wrongfully imprisoned. My lawyer proved my innocence."

"That's cool," said Larry.

Kyle continued to talk. Not much of what he said was truthful. He said he was a truck driver, had been to college, been to about every state, fished in Rio de Janeiro, raced snow machines, dug for potatoes, was engaged to a woman, and worked at a lumberyard in British Columbia. He was trying to impress his new friends. He learned they were involved in criminal activities. This interested Kyle.

He became comfortable around Larry and Greg. He slowly started to talk more about his jail time. He continued to say he was innocent of the crime. They went out drinking and really hit it off. Kyle thought he would be offered a place in their criminal organization. He drove their car when they picked up and dropped off mysterious packages. They never told Kyle what was in those packages, but they paid him after every delivery. He quit his job at the farm because he thought this criminal organization offered a better future with the chance of more money.

Unable to stay at the farm any longer, Kyle was given use of a penthouse suite with a full liquor cabinet. He had a problem with alcohol. With this supply, he started to drink constantly. The treatment he was given impressed him more and more. He continued to insist on his innocence every time Larry and Greg raised the topic.

Soon, Kyle was introduced to the head of the criminal organization. His name was Big Larry. They met at Big Larry's apartment in Winnipeg. At their first meeting, Kyle was offered beer in tall cans, which he drank quickly. Kyle liked the special treatment.

Early in the discussion, Big Larry said to Kyle, "Larry tells me you whacked somebody. That's fine with me. That's fucking excellent. That's the kind of person I'm looking for."

At this time, Kyle had not admitted any guilt to Big Larry, Little Larry, or Greg. Kyle did not correct Big Larry's statement, though.

Kyle continued to be impressed. They flashed rolls of cash in front of him. They made criminal dealings in his presence. Kyle stayed in his first hotel with his new friends. It was in that hotel room that Kyle wondered out loud to Little Larry if it was the right time to tell Big Larry about the murder. Larry repeated an earlier warning: "Don't lie to Big Larry since honesty and loyalty are important to him."

The next time they met with Big Larry, Kyle said he killed Brigitte Grenier. He thought this murder would impress Big Larry. Kyle wanted to look like a guy this organization needed. He hoped to obtain more work and bigger sums of money.

Kyle went to the festival site with Big Larry, Little Larry, and Greg. He described how he killed Brigitte. He got many of the details wrong about how she had actually died. He said he didn't look like the muddy murderer because he had a change of clothes at his friend's house. He went there to change after he killed her.

"Did you just hide the clothes at this guy's place?" asked Big Larry.

"Well, I put it in a bag and stuck it under the bridge, and on my way home that night, after everything was over, I went and grabbed it on my way through."

"Where did you stick 'em overnight?"

"Just coming outta Roseisle, we got a creek and there's a bridge there."

"So then you came back, eh?"

"Yeah, came back right away."

He continued with his detail of the murder. This included hitting her in the head with a stick. Big Larry questioned him.

"How many times did you have to smack her to make sure she's dead?" asked Big Larry.

"I hit her once, seriously, I did," replied Kyle. "But the police seem to think there's two people involved from what I've seen in court. I think there is two people involved."

"You seem to think there's two people involved," said Greg.

"I think there is from the evidence I seen in court. They had evidence saying that there's two people involved. I've seen the pictures. They showed me pictures of the body in the courtroom. She was beaten pretty bad."

"Well, I'll level with you right now," said Big Larry. "I did a little checking on you, 'cause business is business. The murder doesn't sound like what you're saying. Are you bullshitting me?" challenged Big Larry.

"No, no," answered Kyle. "Like I mentioned, there's another guy arrested 'cause they think someone else did it."

"I don't give a fuck about the other guy arrested. Did you kill this broad or not?"

"I think I did," said Kyle, "'cause I gave her a good whoop on the head. And she turned up the next day dead."

"But you think there's a second guy?" asked Larry. "You're trying to tell me that after you did her, somebody else went after and just beat her for the fun of it?"

"Yeah, well, I don't know what happened after I left."

"See, the main thing there, Kyle, is that we gotta make sure all the details are correct, okay?" said Greg.

"I'd like to know who I'm talking to. And right now, it starts to give me a little bit of a bad feeling," said Big Larry, who was looking for somebody he could trust.

Big Larry and Greg left, leaving Larry with Kyle.

"It just didn't look too terribly good," said Kyle. "He didn't seem too impressed with me."

"What do you think they didn't look too impressed about?"

"Well, I guess he figures there's more to it than he sees."

"What did I tell you about a week ago," said Little Larry. "The only thing not to do."

"Bullshit him," replied Kyle.

Kyle said he was worried to tell the story to the wrong people and get sent back to jail. With this on his mind, he wondered why Big Larry would be so concerned with the details. Kyle was also worried he was being recruited to be an assassin. He told Larry he was not interested in killing people. Larry told Kyle not to worry because his organization didn't do that.

This meeting with Big Larry was on June 23, 1991, the one-year anniversary of Brigitte's murder. It was just a coincidence their meeting happened on this date. There was a multi-page article on the murder in a Winnipeg newspaper. While in the truck, returning from the murder scene, Little Larry had Kyle read the article. He wanted to hear all the details. This attention excited Kyle.

"I made history," said Kyle after reading the article. "How many people do you know make history?"

On the same day, Kyle talked with his friend John Beckett. He told him that he had obtained a trusted position within a criminal organization and would be making a lot of money. He said he got the job because of the reputation he had gained as a result of being charged for murder.

Kyle met with Big Larry a third time, on July 25. He wanted to impress him and not have the boss doubt his loyalty. For Big Larry, trust and loyalty would be gained by telling the whole story. These guys wanted the whole story from Kyle. He was ready to give it to impress his new boss.

Kyle's story about the murder evolved. He needed a story to impress Big Larry. He said he acted alone and that Tim Houlahan was innocent. He didn't hit Brigitte once, but many times. He said his muddy and bloody clothes were in an Alberta landfill, said the stick he beat her with was thrown in the creek and floated away. He gave them every detail he could come up with. He thought back to the trial and the newspaper articles he had read about the murder. But, he still got facts wrong.

Kyle told the story about a footbridge that was somehow involved in the murder and about having a car at the festival. He said he took forensic science in high school and that was why he made sure there was no evidence against him at the crime scene.

The three guys sounded like they enjoyed hearing how Kyle killed Brigitte. They continually asked for more detail. Kyle didn't hesitate to give them what they wanted to hear. Some facts on the case were right, while many others were wrong.

Later that same day, Big Larry and his associates picked up Kyle. They said they were going into Carberry. They talked all the way into town. They pulled up to a hotel and said to Kyle they were going in for a beer. Kyle stayed in the car. Minutes later, a man came up to the car.

"Kyle Unger?" asked the man.

"Yeah."

"You wanna step outside, please. Put your hands on the window," ordered the man, who told Kyle he was an

RCMP officer. "You're under arrest for murder. Do you understand that?"

"Yes, I do," said Kyle.

"Do you understand that you're under arrest for the murder of Brigitte Grenier?"

"Yes, I do."

Kyle's Charter rights were read to him and he was placed in police custody. Kyle's three friends, Big Larry, Larry, and Greg, never returned to the car.

11

CHAPTER ELEVEN

OPERATION DRIFTER

How did Kyle find himself in custody again, charged with the murder of Brigitte Grenier for the second time? Turns out, Kyle had been the main character in a make-believe story. It was called "Mr. Big sting." He'd played his part too well. It had cost him his freedom.

The story unfolded like a scene from a Hollywood movie. A criminal organization came along with an opportunity Kyle found hard to resist. They flashed money and power in front of their target. He did and said whatever he had to become part of it.

In a Mr. Big sting operation, most of the actors are undercover police. The only one who isn't aware of the sting is the one who plays the main role: the target. If things work out, the target delivers his lines and the police get the confession they want.

In all Mr. Big sting cases, the target is a suspect in an

ongoing investigation, but there isn't enough evidence to convict the suspect. Undercover police initiate contact with the target with the intention of luring him into a fabricated criminal organization. The purpose is to extract a confession, at all costs, in order to close the case.

Alcohol is often used to seduce the target into participating in criminal activity. The RCMP use various tactics to show their suspect the promise of financial gain, power, and respect within the organization. The goal is for the target to eventually become part of the criminal organization. The police socialize the target into a life of crime. They encourage and promote criminal activity. Other countries refer to these tactics as entrapment. The technique is banned in countries like the United States and United Kingdom. This is because it has led to false confessions and wrongful convictions.

Once the target has joined the organization, they are constantly reminded of how trust is essential within the organization. They stress that lies will never be tolerated, especially by the crime boss, "Mr. Big." In a Mr. Big sting, the RCMP create a real-world criminal environment. They make it nearly impossible for their target to know this fantasy from reality. The target is encouraged to believe that there is real opportunity to be successful in the criminal organization.

The finale of the operation occurs when the target meets Mr. Big. He asks the target about his criminal past, hoping that he will voluntarily confess to the crime. If the target doesn't confess right away, Mr. Big pushes for a confession. He promises that his organization will take care of the legal problems and keep the target out of prison. Under these conditions, the target often confesses.

Kyle played the part of the target perfectly. Big Larry, Larry, and Greg, all undercover police officers, played their parts well, too. They posed as free-spending gang members and lured Kyle into confessing a crime. After just over a week of meetings, Kyle was arrested and charged with the murder of Brigitte Grenier.

This Mr. Big sting was called Operation Drifter. It involved thirteen RCMP officers and was run by Constable Kathleen King. Even though Kyle's original charges were stayed, the RCMP never gave up on their theory. They still thought Kyle was somehow involved in Brigitte's slaying. Kyle himself was unaware he was still a suspect.

After Kyle was originally released from the jail where he had been held prior to the preliminary hearing, the RCMP interviewed inmates who had been in jail with him. They wanted to know if Kyle had confessed to any-body while in jail. One of the inmates they contacted was Jeffrey Cohen. RCMP officers interviewed Cohen in May 1991 at a drug and alcohol rehab program. Cohen didn't remember Kyle's name, but he recognized his picture. He insisted Kyle had confessed to the grisly crime before being released from the Winnipeg Remand Centre on December 11, 1990. He quoted Kyle as telling him, "I killed her and I got away with it." After hearing this, police thought that if Kyle believed he was in the presence of criminals, like in a Mr. Big sting operation, he might actually say what went on that night.

And Kyle did talk.

With his arrest, Kyle was once again in the news. He was once again seen as the monster that murdered Brigitte Grenier. It all happened so fast. When he was arrested, there was no mention to the media of the Mr. Big sting. People wouldn't know until the trial what lengths the RCMP had gone to in order to prove Kyle's guilt. Tim Houlahan was still free on bail, waiting for a trial date. He still wasn't feeling the effects of being charged with first-degree murder.

12

CHAPTER TWELVE

GOING TO TRIAL

The criminal justice system, in its most basic form, involves the state using its resources against the accused. Because of the danger found in such a power imbalance, numerous legal protections have been put in place to ensure fairness. To reduce the risk of imprisoning the innocent, a prosecutor must prove guilt beyond a reasonable doubt.

"Beyond a *reasonable* doubt" means that the suspect's guilt is not merely speculated, unsupported by logic, exaggerated, or only remotely possible. Members of a jury are told to avoid forming opinions too soon. An accused person must be first considered not guilty. The law presumes each accused to be not guilty until the jury decides otherwise.

Kyle was at a disadvantage before the trial even started. He had long been the public face of the crime. And, such a horrible, brutal killing of a young girl made it hard for people, like jurors, to maintain the presumption of innocence for the accused.

The first-degree murder trial began on January 20, 1992 in Winnipeg at the Court of Queen's Bench. Kyle and Tim were on trial together. *Her Majesty the Queen vs. Kyle Wayne Unger and Timothy Lawrence Houlahan.* Kyle and Tim were the defendants. They were aged twenty and eighteen. Both of the accused pleaded not guilty to the charges.

By the time of the trial, Tim was not protected under the *Young Offenders Act* anymore, and he had been raised to the adult court. His name and picture were made public. People were surprised by Tim's involvement. Some didn't think he could have done it. He was the relative unknown at the trial. All eyes were on Kyle.

This was a trial by jury. Eight men and four women were called to decide Tim's and Kyle's fate. "It is a team system where you are the judge of the facts and I am the judge of the laws," said Chief Justice Benjamin Hewak to the jury. "There are two other basic legal principles which are fundamental to your role as jurors. They are the requirement for proof beyond a reasonable doubt and the presumption of not guilty."

George Dangerfield led the Crown's case. He was one of the most successful Crown attorneys in Manitoba history. It was up to him to prove the guilt of the accused beyond a reasonable doubt. Hersh Wolch was originally on Kyle's case, but he was busy with another important case. His law partner Sheldon Pinx was brought in to defend Kyle. It was up to him to argue that the Crown's case was not true. That would give Kyle a ruling by the jury of not guilty.

Brenda Keyser defended Tim at the trial. Both Pinx and Keyser wanted separate trials for their clients. They thought it would give them a better chance against a guilty verdict. Crown prosecutor Dangerfield wanted a joint trial. His theory implied they both had a hand in the murder of Brigitte Grenier. Dangerfield won that first battle. Without separate trials, jurors could hear the full text of Tim Houlahan's confession implicating Unger in the crime. Normally, the statement of a co-accused is not allowed. The only exception is when the prosecutors are lucky enough to keep both accused in front of the same jury.

Pinx and Keyser were not just defending their clients against the Crown's theory. They were also battling each other. They each had to make the other defendant look like the true murderer. If they succeeded, their client might not go to prison.

George Dangerfield opened the trial with the Crown's theory of the murder. He told the jury what he thought happened and what he would try to prove throughout the trial. The prosecution's theory started with an assumption that Kyle Unger was obsessed by the fact that Grenier had rebuffed him while dancing at the festival. He wanted sex and this was working on his mind. By the end of the night, Dangerfield contended, Kyle was looking for Brigitte.

The prosecution also believed that Tim began having consensual sex with Brigitte. Then things started getting out of hand and it turned to rape. Kyle happened on them, saw the situation, and joined in. It was Unger who beat Brigitte, strangled her, and shoved the sticks into her body.

Dangerfield continued with his theory. He claimed that Tim lent a hand, helped carry the body, and put it in the river. He was threatened by Kyle to keep quiet. Kyle changed his clothing. They both went back to their groups of friends.

Dangerfield had to prove this theory to the jury. Pinx had to prove his client was not guilty, partly by making Tim Houlahan look like the murderer.

CHAPTER THIRTEEN

STACKED EVIDENCE

Crown Attorney George Dangerfield made his case by calling on witnesses who attended the festival. They were asked about the events over the course of the evening of the murder. Questions focused on Brigitte, Tim, and Kyle. There were no eyewitnesses to the murder. Tim Houlahan was the only person who claimed to have seen what happened. Dangerfield tried to develop a picture of what went on that evening.

The police had gathered evidence at the murder scene and from suspects. Dangerfield called on the experts who analyzed the evidence and the police who gathered it. The jury members were riveted and visibly shaken by some of the more gruesome details.

Dr. Peter Markesleyn, a forensic pathologist, autopsied the body. He gave all the details of Brigitte's death that he had gathered from examining her body. He said that given the large degree of bruising on her head, she was likely struck with sufficient force to have rendered her unconscious. He found the principal cause of death was strangulation.

Dr. Norman Sperber, a forensic orthodontologist, specialized in bite marks. He testified that Kyle did not make the bite marks on Brigitte's body. He had frequently seen similar bite marks in cases of violent assault. They would have happened when Brigitte was still alive and would have been painful. Tim never gave his bite mark impressions for comparison.

Philip Hodge, a serologist, conducted the blood and body fluid analysis. He testified that blood samples on Tim's clothes were from Brigitte. Blood and alcohol analyst Patricia Lehman testified that Tim, Kyle, and Brigitte had varying blood alcohol levels. It was also found that Kyle had traces of LSD in his system.

Sheldon Pinx, Kyle's lawyer, tried to highlight one major point. How could Kyle have committed the crime when none of the forensic evidence connected him to the crime? At the same time, there was a lot of evidence connecting Tim to the crime. Tim's muddy and blood-covered clothes should have been Kyle's ticket to a not guilty verdict.

The Crown had a few more key witnesses. Dangerfield

called Dr. James Cadieux to the witness stand. He was an expert in hair and fibre comparison, called forensic microscopy. It involves the side-by-side comparison of hair under a microscope. Strands of hair taken from a suspect are compared to strands of hair taken from the crime scene. The objective is to see if the two groups of evidence come from the same source. If there is a match, the suspect must have been at the crime scene.

Cadieux had hair samples from both Tim and Kyle. He compared them to hairs found at the crime scene.

"The conclusion that is drawn is that the questioned hair is consistent with having originated from the same sources as the known samples," testified Cadieux. He said the hair found on Brigitte's sweatshirt was consistent with hair samples provided by Kyle. Other hairs found were consistent with Tim.

Normally, witnesses are not allowed to give an opinion. The scientific nature of Cadieux's testimony was potentially damaging to Kyle.

Tim's presence at the crime scene was proven by evidence and admitted to by his lawyer. The hair analysis became the Crown's only forensic evidence to link Kyle to the murder. Cadieux's credentials and his ability to recognize matching hairs impressed the jury.

The next big turn against Kyle came when jailhouse

informant Jeffrey Cohen took the stand. He said he had no motive to lie and was promised nothing in exchange for testifying. He testified that while they were in jail together, he had overheard Kyle admitting he had "gotten away with murder."

Cohen was cross-examined by Pinx. "You think this jury will believe you're a trustworthy individual?" Pinx asked Cohen, after reading to the jury his lengthy twenty-seven-year criminal record. Cohen shot back, challenging Pinx, "I hope they do, unless you can prove otherwise. Why would I make up a story like that? Answer that — I don't think you can." Pinx asked Cohen if he was aware that Kyle maintained his innocence to twenty-one other inmates. "That's the stupidest question I've ever heard in my life," Cohen said with disgust. Pinx found a video showing Kyle was not in the cell when the informant said he overheard the confession. It was up to the jury to decide if Cohen was a credible witness.

The key to the Crown's case against Kyle was the Mr. Big sting. It wasn't just a hair found on a sweatshirt or a jailhouse informant. They also had Kyle on tape confessing to brutally killing Brigitte. Most people outside the RCMP did not know the details of Operation Drifter. That secret was made public at the trial. Dangerfield used it to portray Kyle as a monster.

Dangerfield called on the undercover officers to test-ify on the witness stand. They told the jury what went on during the undercover operation. They read out Kyle's confession of how he murdered Brigitte. One of the undercover RCMP officers started to cry while reading out the details.

It got very emotional in the courtroom. The jury was disgusted by what they heard. The police were proud to have caught Kyle the way they did. They had gotten him to confess to the crime. "The public watching in the gallery mostly would have skipped the trial and gone straight to hanging," reported one Winnipeg newspaper after the RCMP brought forward Kyle's confession.

It was up to Sheldon Pinx to prove Kyle's innocence to the jury. It wasn't going to be easy.

Brigitte Grenier was sixteen when she was murdered at the Woodstick Music Festival near Roseisle, Manitoba in June 1990. Her picture appeared on the front of the *Winnipeg Sun* on June 26, 1990. *Winnipeg Sun.*

RCMP Constable Ron Muir stands near the muddy creek where Brigitte Grenier's body was found. David Johnson, *Winnipeg Free Press*.

Crown prosecutor George Dangerfield had several wrongful convictions attached to his name. Wayne Glowacki, *Winnipeg Free Press*.

Kyle and his father made the front page of the *Winnipeg Sun* on December 10, 1990, when Kyle was released following his preliminary hearing. *Winnipeg Sun.*

Kyle's trial lawyer, Sheldon Pinx, speaking to the media following the 1991 trial. Phil Hossack, *Winnipeg Free Press*.

UNGER, 20, CHARGED IN MURDER - AGAIN 3

RCMP reinstate charges in year-old Grenier slaying

THE VICTIM: Brigitte Grenier   THE CO-ACCUSED: Kyle Unger

The June 27, 1991, front page of the *Winnipeg Sun* when Kyle was recharged with Brigitte's death following his confession to undercover police officers. *Winnipeg Sun*.

Kyle's murder trial was followed closely by the newspapers, espeically the *Winnipeg Sun*. *Winnipeg Sun*.

Kyle and his mother, Treva Unger, speak to the press following Kyle's acquittal in 2009. Wayne Glowacki, *Winnipeg Free Press*.

Kyle, with his lawyer Hersch Wolch on left, said it took nearly twenty years to get his life back. Ken Gigliotti, *Winnipeg Free Press*.

14

CHAPTER FOURTEEN

PROVING HIS INNOCENCE

Dangerfield had done his job well. His theory of who killed Brigitte Grenier was thoroughly supported by the witnesses and evidence he presented. In order for Kyle to have a chance, Pinx had to tear apart the evidence at trial. He had to make the evidence look less credible.

Pinx tried to discredit Cohen as a witness. Then he tried to show the jury that Kyle was a "bullshitter" who often made up stories. This was especially important to establish when it came to Kyle's confession in Operation Drifter. Pinx had his chance to do this when he cross-examined the undercover officers. He questioned how Kyle seemed transformed over the nine days between meeting the undercover officers and confessing to the crime. The lawyer suggested that enticements from the RCMP undercover team had something to do with it.

"When you met him, he was a young farm boy from

the Hickory Hollow Hobby Farm. He's come quite a way in nine days, hasn't he?" Pinx asked when he cross-examined the key undercover operator to whom Kyle had confessed. Pinx suggested Kyle was in awe of Big Larry and his money. "He often asked what kind of an impression he'd made on Big Larry, didn't he?" Pinx asked Constable Larry Tremblay.

Tremblay denied Kyle was ever offered a job, but he admitted they conveyed the idea that they were criminals who made a lot of money. They brought him meals and cigarettes and flashed money in front of him. Kyle was excited when they put him in a fancy hotel. But Tremblay flatly denied he tried to make Kyle "correct" his confession because his details didn't match what happened the night Brigitte died.

When Pinx was finished cross-examining the undercover officers, Crown Attorney Dangerfield didn't have any other witnesses to call to the stand.

Now it was Sheldon Pinx's turn. In his opening statement, Pinx said that although his client gave graphic "disgusting murder confessions to undercover officers," Unger was "only saying what he thought they wanted to hear."

"Kyle Unger is indeed a liar, he's a braggart, he likes to impress people," Pinx continued. "What Kyle Unger told police was what they wanted to hear — no question — but it was not the truth. Criminals are bad people, bad people do bad things and they say bad things — it's our theory Kyle Unger wanted to be one of these bad people."

It was time for Pinx to call his own witnesses in Kyle's defence. The first witness he called to the stand shocked the audience. Heads jerked up and mouths were agape as defence attorney Sheldon Pinx announced Kyle Unger would take the witness box in his own defence.

The courtroom was silent and all eyes were on Kyle, as the slight, twenty-year-old with long, dark hair and a moustache made his way to the stand after the sheriff's officer removed his shackles.

After swearing on a Bible, Kyle told the jury he wasn't responsible for Brigitte Grenier's murder in June 1990.

"Kyle, did you kill Brigitte Grenier?" Pinx asked.

"No, I never," Kyle replied in a calm, deep monotone voice.

"Were you at the scene of her death?"

"No, I wasn't."

Unger told the court he had been lying when he gave the graphic murder confession to the RCMP officers who posed as criminals. "I hoped to receive employment, large amounts of money, and acceptance into their group," Kyle said, explaining why he had confessed. He said he was shocked and it kind of scared him when an undercover cop said, "So, you whacked somebody. That's great, that's excellent." He went along, not wanting to ruin his chances of a job, he explained.

Kyle rigidly stuck to that explanation when grilled by Tim's lawyer, Brenda Keyser, and Crown Attorney George Dangerfield. He told Dangerfield he'd heard the information he gave in his confessions during his preliminary hearing. Dangerfield suggested only Kyle could have known the graphic details.

"You were telling a story about how you held her head steady and smacked her with a stick because you're the one who did it," Dangerfield said.

"That's incorrect," Kyle calmly replied.

Dangerfield persisted. "The fact is you were angry at Brigitte Grenier because she turned you down and you went looking for her and discovered her and Houlahan in a fight and you jumped in and you killed her and you and Houlahan dragged the body in the creek."

Unger replied, "That's incorrect."

In her cross-examination, Keyser hammered at Kyle's credibility. She suggested he lied so often, he didn't know the truth. "How can you assure the jury you're not lying now?" Keyser asked.

"There's no way I can convince them. I hope they'll believe me because I'm under oath," Kyle replied.

Keyser suggested he was "acting" on the witness stand by cleaning up his language and using vocabulary he normally wouldn't use.

People were surprised Kyle took the stand. Pinx was counting on it to prove his client's innocence after the jury heard the undercover operation confession.

After Kyle, no more witnesses took the stand. Tim remained silent throughout the trial. Dangerfield and Pinx were never given a chance to ask him questions during cross-examination. The jury only heard the statements he gave the police. All that remained of the trial were the lawyers' closing statements and the final verdict.

15

CHAPTER FIFTEEN

CLOSING STATEMENT: PINX

While preparing for his closing statement, Sheldon Pinx kicked around various ideas and approaches to get the jurors to actually step back and look at the evidence. He didn't want them to make their decision by emotion alone. Pinx and his team came up with a plan. They didn't just want to show Kyle was not guilty. They wanted to paint a picture to the jury of who might be the murderer.

There was only one way for Kyle to avoid wrongful conviction at the end of the trial. His counsel had to use that opportunity. Pinx seized the chance during his closing statement in defence of Kyle.

"Members of the jury, Brigitte Grenier's killer is sitting in this courtroom. There he sits, Tim Houlahan, whose lawyer I expect will have you believe that he sat and watched while Brigitte Grenier was brutally murdered.

"The loudest witness in this courtroom was the

silence of Tim Houlahan. Why didn't he take the witness stand and try to explain to each and every one of you his conduct after he left that dance floor with Brigitte Grenier, his conduct in the face of damning physical evidence against him? And why didn't he tell us under oath, 'I didn't kill Brigitte Grenier'?

"Members of the jury, the answer is simple. It's the same reason he didn't provide teeth samples to the police. He's afraid to get into that box and answer questions.

"Explain, Mr. Houlahan, because you can't, how in fact was it that you got covered in mud? How did you get that blood on your shoe consistent with that of Brigitte Grenier? How did you get the scratches on your face? How did you get those scratches on your hands?

"How is it that, as we expect, your lawyer is going to tell us you were beaten, you had only a couple of little, minor bruises on your face?

"Members of the jury, think of that question and think of the answer you didn't get from that box. Unger gave teeth, blood, and hair samples for the police. Houlahan didn't. Unger had nothing to hide.

"Some people, because of the way they speak and sound and the way they described in a horrible way the ending of a life of another human, can enrage us all. That gets us all angry and, rightfully so, we get mad. We get

mad, we get angry, we get disgusted, but please, remember, we don't convict people because they may or may
not look guilty.

"There is no prototype or model of a killer.

"Don't get confused and mistaken by appearances.
This is not perhaps the best-kept looking young man that
you may have ever seen by any means, but that is Kyle
Unger. Police wanted to believe what Jeff Cohen said.
The Crown wanted to believe what he said. It's exactly
what they wanted to hear.

"Perhaps I've never been in this position before as a
lawyer; to convince you of my client's innocence, I have
to convince you he's a liar.

"Mr. Big police are some of the cleverest people. The
scheme is to make Kyle believe that he has a chance of
becoming part of this little criminal organization. He's
a twenty-year-old young man who saw an opportunity
to make some money. Out of work, just out of jail a few
months before, having trouble finding work.

"Three times he told the undercover police he was
innocent.

"Members of the jury, so much of what Kyle has told
the police is factually incorrect. In fact, the proven facts
prove he is not telling the truth. And Kyle told you why
he wasn't telling the truth. He was trying to impress and

trying to get a job. He was duped into thinking that there are things he had to say in order to make them think that this was the person they were looking for.

"People testified he was wearing the same clothes all night. But we sure wanted to believe he changed his clothes. Don't we want to believe that? We do because it makes him guilty. We want to believe it because it makes him guilty, because that's the only feasible explanation as to why Unger didn't have anything on his clothes, any mud or blood or dirt or hair."

Pinx did his best to make Tim Houlahan look like Brigitte Grenier's killer. Would Tim's silence make him look like he had something to hide? Pinx sat down and waited to hear what the other lawyers had to say.

16

CHAPTER SIXTEEN

CLOSING STATEMENT: KEYSER

After Pinx, Brenda Keyser gave her closing remarks in the defence of Tim Houlahan. She started by describing reasonable doubt to the jury.

"Burden is on the Crown to prove Houlahan's guilt and it has to be based on evidence," said Keyser to the jury. "Pinx wants you to speculate on Houlahan's guilt. Tim Houlahan didn't say he killed Brigitte Grenier at any time.

"Crown said Kyle Unger beat her, shoved sticks into her and that Kyle Unger killed her," Keyser continued. "The Crown is not saying that Tim Houlahan beat Brigitte Grenier, strangled Brigitte Grenier, or shoved sticks into Brigitte Grenier's body. The best they can do is to say he helped carry the body to the creek.

"Tim Houlahan tells you that he was forced to hit Brigitte Grenier twice. It's the killer's twisted way of making Tim Houlahan part of the murder so that he would be silenced. Unger would lie to get a job, but he wouldn't lie to stay out of jail?

"I'm sure some of you also may have been surprised that Tim didn't take the box and tell you what happened," said Keyser, who followed up by stating he didn't have to get in the witness stand because his side of the story was told in his statements to the police.

"Kyle Unger had to take the stand because he had to undo what he had said before. That's the very big difference between Kyle Unger and Tim Houlahan. It's not up to Tim to prove to you that he's innocent; that's not the way it works. It's not his job or his burden or his onus, it's the Crown's, pure and simple.

"Tim Houlahan tells you Kyle Unger killed Brigitte Grenier. Kyle Unger confessed to doing just that, and Mr. Pinx is very right, the killer is right here in the courtroom. He's right there," said Keyser, pointing at Kyle. "Now I say to you that Kyle Unger has had enough perverse pleasure out of the nightmare. He's already taken one life; don't let him take another."

17

CHAPTER SEVENTEEN

CLOSING STATEMENT: DANGERFIELD

Crown Attorney George Dangerfield was the last lawyer to give closing remarks. He was in a very powerful position. He was the last person the jurors would hear in the courtroom before they made a decision. He had already proved a solid case against Kyle and Tim. His closing remarks had to cement their guilt in the jurors' minds.

Dangerfield was a tall, distinguished prosecutor with piercing blue eyes, a quick wit, and a great, believable presence. He was a courthouse favourite, deeply admired by police, the judiciary, and even the defence. He liked to put on a show for the jury. He wove a tale and presented the closing as his final act.

"It cannot be overemphasized that the purpose of a criminal prosecution is not to obtain a conviction, it is to lay before a jury what the Crown considers to be credible evidence relevant to what is alleged to be a crime.

Counsel have a duty to see that all available legal proof of the facts is presented," said Dangerfield to the jury.

It was in the public's interest for him to achieve a just result. They wanted somebody to go to jail and be labelled as the murderer. Tim and Kyle should have been considered innocent before guilty. But Dangerfield was convinced they were both guilty. He built his case to show their guilt. He went on to give the jury his theory of the killing.

Dangerfield said that the bite marks, scratches, and bruises came as Grenier tried to ward off Tim's assault. Then the violence escalated.

"Tim Houlahan wanted her dead," Dangerfield said. "If she died, she couldn't report him for the attack."

Dangerfield then talked about Kyle.

"Unger was obsessed with Grenier after being rebuffed by her, and it was his rage and Houlahan's fear that killed her.

"Unger's admission to police posing as a criminal gang may not perfectly match evidence, but they make sense," he said. "Unger knew the criminals didn't want police attention, so he didn't tell them Tim Houlahan witnessed the crime, and he wanted to seem tough, so he changed facts to make himself look better."

Dangerfield said it would be up to the jury to decide whether Unger was just making up the stories to impress the gang or whether he did what he said he did.

"It was to be an evening of fun, drinking, dancing, listening to music, tenting, campfires, the sort of summer fun one would expect would be indulged in Manitoba in that area. No one going to it expected a murder.

"People came and went as they pleased. So, there was nothing about the evening so startling as to draw anyone's attention to time, place, events, people, or anything."

Dangerfield was trying to lead the jury away from witness testimony. He wanted them to instead focus on physical evidence found at the scene of the crime. The police confessions by Kyle were also important to his case.

The Crown took the position that Houlahan and Brigitte Grenier were introduced to one another during the course of the evening at the Woodstick Music Festival. They seemed to hit it off to the point where they were dancing together very closely, kissing, and that, ultimately, they went off together into the area of the creek to continue a necking session and some of her clothing was removed consensually.

The Crown suggested that things got out of hand and that Houlahan persisted with his sexual advances, but that Brigitte Grenier refused to go any further. Because of that, a disagreement between Grenier and Houlahan arose. Then Unger came upon the scene.

Dangerfield said that because Unger had been rebuffed by Brigitte Grenier earlier, he became angry and began to tear Brigitte's clothing, beat her, and strangle her. He was joined in this beating by Houlahan, and they both beat her and then dumped her body in the creek.

The Crown said that the biting of Brigitte Grenier and the tearing off of her clothes was sexual assault. The assault continued until Brigitte Grenier was choked and beaten to death by Unger and Houlahan. On that basis, the Crown took the position that they were both guilty of first-degree murder.

Dangerfield was done with his closing remarks. New witnesses or evidence could not be presented to the jury. It was up to the jury to process all the information presented to them. The futures of the co-accused lay in the decision of the jury.

18

CHAPTER EIGHTEEN

NO CHANCE FOR PAROLE

The judge made a charge to the jury before they went into seclusion to make their decision.

"Decide this case only on the evidence that you have heard in the courtroom and not on any other basis," said Queen's Bench Court Judge Hewak. "You are the sole judge of the facts in the case.

"To bring in a true verdict according to the evidence, that means that you should only consider the testimony and the exhibits which have come before you at this trial. You must put out of your mind all prejudice and all sympathy, which you may have on anything you may have heard or read or seen. Significant because of the very emotional nature of this case."

. . .

"Consider the case and the evidence as it applies to each man separately. Each accused must be treated as if he were being tried separately for the offence charged."

Kyle's future rested on reasonable doubt, explained the judge.

"If you believe the testimony of Unger — you must acquit. If you do not believe the testimony of the accused Unger, but you are left in a reasonable doubt by it — you must acquit.

"Even if you are not left in doubt by the testimony of the accused Unger, you must ask yourself whether on the basis of all the evidence which you do accept, you are convinced beyond a reasonable doubt by that evidence of the guilt of the accused Unger. If you are so convinced, then you may convict him. On the other hand, if you have a reasonable doubt, then you must acquit.

"The matter, members of the jury, is now in your hands. Your decision must be unanimous."

★ ★ ★

After fifteen hours, the jury came to a decision. The courtroom was full of family and friends of both the victim and those accused. The only notable absence was Kyle's parents.

Brigitte's sister, Mariette, burst into tears as the jury came into the room. Agnes Grenier, Brigitte's mother, clutched her husband's arm; a weak smile crossed her face as the jury foreman delivered the verdict. Ron Grenier sat on the edge of his seat, his fists tensed and his knuckles white, until the verdict was read and relief flooded his face.

Both of the accused stared ahead blankly as the jury announced it had found them both guilty of first-degree murder. It was a conviction carrying a life sentence with no chance of parole for twenty-five years.

The reactions of the accused were in stark contrast to that of Tim Houlahan's parents. His mother, Linda, sobbing as she entered the courtroom, appeared stunned when the jury announced her son's fate. Afterward, she expressed only rage.

"Don't you know what we've been through this whole time ... how could the jury say he was guilty with the evidence they had," she said, as the family looked for a way out of the building, away from the glare of television cameras.

Even Houlahan's lawyer, Brenda Keyser, broke down with tears.

The justice system tells us an accused person is presumed innocent until proven guilty — except when that person is accused of a horrific murder of an attractive teenager. In those cases, relief trumps common sense.

That sense of relief filled the case; remained all through the trial.

The evidence against Kyle was expertly examined by lawyer Sheldon Pinx's breakdown of the case against his client. He showed the jailhouse informant was not trustworthy. The confession to undercover RCMP officers should not be trusted. He argued for the jury to see Tim Houlahan as the murderer and not Kyle, based on the physical evidence presented against him. The problem was nobody listened. The need to hold someone accountable, along with the lust for relief, appeared to have clouded the jury's judgment.

The province felt the relief of convicting somebody for its most gruesome murder. Brigitte Grenier's parents started to feel a sense of closure. Not necessarily relief or joy, just closure. At least now they had some sense of what happened to their daughter and who was responsible.

Kyle was shocked by the jury's decision. He thought there would be a reasonable doubt as to whether he was guilty or not. He wasn't ready to stop fighting for his future as an innocent man.

19

CHAPTER NINETEEN

LAST CHANCE FOR FREEDOM

Both Kyle and Tim appealed the court's conviction and sentence. If either person won his appeal, he would be released from jail. He would have a chance to prove his innocence at another trial. They both asserted their innocence. They both wanted to be free from jail.

In his appeal, Kyle's lawyer argued that the method used by the police officers — the Mr. Big sting — relied on dirty tricks and entrapment, and that the undercover scenario was unfair. However, the Manitoba Court of Appeal found that Unger's statements of confession were admissible because they were not made to persons of authority. The undercover police officers were not considered persons of authority, as the accused was not aware of their true identity.

The Manitoba Court of Appeal was critical of Pinx and the closing statement he had made at the trial. They said Pinx had pointed the finger too strenuously at Houlahan and tried to get the jury to understand that acquitting Unger did not mean that the killer would go free. The jury didn't buy it and convicted both men.

The Court of Appeal's criticism of Pinx's statement formed the basis on which a new trial was ordered for Houlahan but not Unger. The Court of Appeal framed this part of its decision as part of what it considered a miscarriage of justice. They thought the decision not to have separate trials resulted in an unfair trial for Houlahan.

Houlahan's appeal was allowed and a new trial was ordered. He was set free on bail.

The Manitoba Court of Appeal dismissed Kyle's appeal against conviction on July 7, 1992. He tried to make an appeal to the Supreme Court of Canada. His application was dismissed on December 2, 1993. There were no other ways for Kyle to overturn the ruling. He was incarcerated in a federal institution. He would not be eligible for parole until 2016.

While out of jail waiting for a new trial, Tim Houlahan committed suicide. He was twenty-one years old. People said the stress of the situation brought him to kill himself. The charges against him were stayed. He wasn't innocent or guilty. Throughout the process, Tim never faced the same hardship as Kyle. When Kyle was waiting for the trial in jail, Tim got to live a normal life. Kyle was the face of the murder, and he was the most hated person in Manitoba. The *Young Offenders Act* had protected Tim before the trial, so he was the relative unknown when it started. It will never be known if Tim was truly guilty of the crime. If he was guilty, Tim would never pay for his actions. Kyle would be in jail for the next twenty-five years for a crime he said he didn't commit.

CHAPTER TWENTY

LIFE BEHIND BARS

Kyle was twenty years old when he started his life sentence at the Stony Mountain Penitentiary in Manitoba. After six months at Stony, he was transferred to a prison in Edmonton, Alberta. It would be unthinkable what he would go through in prison.

"The last time I saw the sunlight was when they drove me from the Law Courts building to Stony Mountain prison, and then two years later, I saw the light again when I got transferred to Alberta. At that point, when I seen the light, it was the beginning of what's ahead of me . . . what's ahead of me was a whole life of concrete and steel and behind me is to say goodbye to everything that was dear to me.

"So it was the beginning of the goodbye."

Kyle's sentence included super-maximum security, which meant 23 hours and 50 minutes per day in lock-up.

"I shut my life down and closed off to any emotion, and feeling, and I lost myself on 24-hour lock-up."

The ten minutes outside of his cell were used for activities like showering.

"My cell had no windows. They could have played a joke on me by bringing me breakfast at seven at night, and I would think it was in the morning. I never seen the light for two years."

The two years in Edmonton were his most difficult.

"People will stab you there to try out a new knife."

The most terrifying moments in prison included riots, when he feared for his life.

"I barricaded myself off in my cell to stay alive. You can smell smoke and flame and blood all around you. All you hear is screaming and crying around you. All you hear are gunshots around you from the guards on the catwalks with the shotguns. All you see are the flashing lights through your window from the flames burning. And you hope the flames go out and the killing stops before they get to you."

During Kyle's first month at Edmonton, his cellmate slit his throat with a razor during the night.

"I woke up in the morning all sticky, thinking I spilled coffee on me with sugar. I turned the lights on and it was his blood that drained out all over me, all over the mattress. That was my first experience of death, wearing his blood from head to toe, literally tasting it."

Kyle's parents, Wayne and Treva, were deeply affected by their son's imprisonment. His mother spent time in the hospital, worn down by stress. They were devoted to him. They believed in their son's innocence.

When Kyle was transferred to a British Columbia prison, his parents pulled up their stakes in Manitoba. His parents, both retired, sold their home to follow him. They visited him in jail two to four times a month.

"Took us years to build that place. My father didn't waste a minute. Instantly a 'For Sale' sign, got the money, packed up everything they owned in a U-Haul, and rented a place," said Kyle.

Kyle became a drug user in jail. His parents helped him kick that habit. He considered suicide while in prison. His love for his parents prevented him from taking his own life.

"I wanted to kill myself every day, but I could not put my parents through that. Not with the support they gave me. How can you give up on someone that doesn't give up on you?"

Kyle took every opportunity to do programs that would prepare him for life outside. It was also a way to avoid the negative effects of jail, especially the violence that was all around him.

"Inmates often give up because they have no one to keep them going. My parents were very supportive. They were part of my survival, my strength, and my serenity."

Kyle took various college courses while in jail. He developed an interest in woodcarving. A local British Columbia artist became his mentor. After a while, Kyle's artwork could be found in Vancouver art galleries. By 2003, he had spent his entire adult life in jail. He still had another thirteen years until he was eligible for parole. That didn't mean he would get released at that time. But that was his only possible hope. All avenues of appeal had been used up.

It would take special circumstances for the justice department to review the case.

21

CHAPTER TWENTY-ONE

DNA UNDER REVIEW

The only piece of physical evidence tying Kyle to the murder was a single hair found on Brigitte's Nike sweatshirt. The hair was identified by microscopic comparison as belonging to Kyle. Hair comparison, once used regularly to tie accused people to murder scenes, had come under attack after DNA testing had proved it wrong.

The policing community placed considerable emphasis on hair microscopy. The RCMP had thirty-five hair comparison experts across Canada. Prosecutors relied upon it in court, primarily to help establish the identity of the suspect in a murder case. It would soon be considered nothing but an educated guess.

All this was brought home to Manitoba by the case of convicted murderer James Driskell. In 2002 and 2003, counsel for Driskell conducted a reinvestigation of his case. As part of this, Manitoba Justice arranged for a DNA test of the hair evidence from his case. That test showed that the hair microscopy evidence had been wrong.

Lawyers for the Association in Defence of the Wrongly Convicted (AIDWYC) complained publicly. AIDWYC was formed in 1993. They are a non-profit organization dedicated to reversing wrongful convictions. They complained that despite knowing hair comparison was imperfect, lawyers used it used to sway jurors. AIDWYC lawyer James Lockyer convinced the Manitoba government to examine all the murder convictions that relied on hair comparison evidence.

On April 23, 2003, Bruce MacFarlane, Deputy Minister and Deputy Attorney General for the Province of Manitoba, announced that an advisory committee would be established. It was called the Forensic Evidence Review Committee (FERC). Its mandate was to review homicide cases from the previous fifteen years that had relied upon hair comparison evidence to secure a conviction. FERC's goal was to actually seek out any possible miscarriages of justice that may have resulted from hair comparison evidence. The committee would be given one year to report. They were empowered to do any testing thought necessary to complete the task.

Manitoba was the first province in Canada to do a systematic review of all murder and manslaughter cases where hair comparison evidence was used to secure a conviction. Manitoba did it to ensure the wrongfully convicted did not stay behind bars.

On August 19, 2004, the committee filed its report. They had started with 175 cases. Following their review of trial transcripts, they determined that only two cases qualified to be reinvestigated. Kyle Unger's case was one of them.

Kyle was approached and agreed to provide DNA samples. DNA testing was performed. The results were not surprising to the AIDWYC. The DNA showed that the original microscopy examination was wrong. The hair on Brigitte's sweater did not match Kyle. The committee referred the case back to Manitoba Justice for review, noting that Kyle's case should be given priority attention.

By this time, Kyle had already spent thirteen years in jail for a murder he insisted he did not commit. AIDWYC lawyer James Lockyer made the call to Kyle to tell him the good news. New DNA tests put his conviction into doubt. Kyle learned that freedom may yet be his.

CHAPTER TWENTY-TWO

WRONGFULLY CONVICTED

Although Kyle Unger always maintained his innocence, he didn't believe he would be set free. "When you claim to be innocent, no one takes you seriously, because everyone in jail is 'innocent,'" Kyle said. "But I never stopped trying to prove my innocence."

It was this belief that made his time in prison harder.

"When you claim you're innocent, you have to work extra hard to prove you're a better person."

Kyle now had a way to prove his innocence. Based on the review committee's findings, Kyle's counsel filed an application to the Minister of Justice for a review of his conviction. The application was made under Section 696.1 of the Canadian Criminal Code. The conviction review process was the only path to freedom after a convicted person had exhausted all appeals through the court system. He also applied for release from jail during the review.

On the basis of the committee's report, it was clear that Unger's conviction was insecure. Confidence in the system was at stake. Nobody in the justice system wanted a wrongful conviction. But it was looking as though Kyle never received a fair trial.

It all started when the police formed a theory before they had any evidence. Then they made the facts fit into their theory.

The nearly limitless powers of the state and its police forces are pitted against a defendant represented by an appointed lawyer with limited resources and powers of investigation. Defendants are protected by the assumption of innocence, the right to remain silent, and the requirement that the Crown prove its case beyond a reasonable doubt.

But it is not a perfect system. In Manitoba, there was growing evidence of a pattern of abuse by Crown prosecutors, like Crown Attorney George Dangerfield against Kyle. Assumption of innocence never played a part in some cases. Defendants like Kyle were assumed to be guilty and the Crown wanted a conviction. There was no chance for a fair trial.

Confirmed wrongful convictions are a rare event in the Canadian justice system. They are considered to be the greatest tragedy of the criminal justice system. They are devastating on many levels: for the victim of the crime, whose actual perpetrator escapes justice; for the system itself, which loses credibility; and obviously for the person convicted, whose life is forever changed and, in many ways, destroyed.

AIDWYC lawyers James Lockyer and Hersh Wolch argued for Kyle's release in a Winnipeg court. They argued that three pieces of evidence should be removed from the Crown's case against Kyle. The hair sample, the only physical evidence linking Kyle to the murder scene, should be removed. The testimony of jailhouse inform-ant, Jeffrey Cohen, should be removed. (It was found his testimony was false and would not be used in a modern court of law.) And most important, the confession to RCMP undercover officers should be removed. They could not have gotten permission to do the Mr. Big sting operation without Cohen's testimony, which was full of holes. They continued to argue it was a false confession brought on by unfair police tactics.

On November 4, 2005, Manitoba Court of Queen's Bench Judge Holly Beard ordered that convicted killer Kyle Unger be released on bail because of very serious concerns that he was wrongfully convicted. Justice Beard issued a written decision that freed Kyle on $225,000 bail, pending the final decision of the federal justice minister on whether to order further review or a new trial.

Beard noted in her decision that she found "strong evidence that the applicant's conviction may not be sustainable." She said the Crown had withdrawn two key pieces of evidence — a hair sample and testimony from a jailhouse informant. And a third piece of evidence, Kyle's confession to undercover RCMP officers, was "fraught with serious weakness and is likely to be assessed by an expert in false confession." However, an expert assessment of the confession could take months if not years to complete, and it would be unreasonable to keep Unger in jail until that time, Beard wrote. "If that report concludes that the confession was false, there will be no evidence against Mr. Unger," Beard continued.

This was only the fourth time in Canadian legal history that a convicted murderer had been granted bail. Kyle was a free man, for now.

At the bail hearing, Kyle's parents and uncles showed their devotion to Kyle. They put up cash and a letter of credit required for bail. They also testified on their thoughts and feelings about Kyle. They supported him completely and believed in his innocence.

"I certainly have a lot of confidence in Kyle," said Stan Unger, his uncle. "I love him, I care for him, and

I'm prepared to do whatever I can do to help him in the future."

On November 24, 2005, Kyle was released into the custody of his parents. He was thirty-four years old on release and had spent the previous fourteen years in jail. He had to follow a set of rules while out of jail. He had to keep the peace and be of good behaviour, live with his parents, not consume alcohol or illegal drugs, observe a curfew, and he couldn't get a driver's licence or drive any motor vehicle. He would have to do this until the federal justice minister made a final decision on his case.

23

CHAPTER TWENTY-THREE

STARTING FROM SCRATCH

When he was released, Kyle had every reason to be bitter, but he wasn't. Instead, he said his time served was both good and bad.

"I was a high school dropout when I was arrested," said Kyle, who studied while in jail. "It gave me a wake-up call."

Kyle said the only angry feelings he had about the whole thing were toward Tim Houlahan. He thought everyone else was doing their job, trying to keep people safe.

He moved to Merritt, British Columbia, to live with his parents. He waited to see if the justice system wanted to give him a new trial or give up on prosecuting him. Kyle felt like having a new trial. He hoped a jury would see the real story.

When Kyle was released on bail, he had a lot of time

to reflect on his past. He didn't only lose fourteen years of his life, but also his sense of home.

Treva and Wayne Unger had sold their place in Roseisle when Kyle was moved to a British Columbia prison. They went to be close to him and support him. But Kyle missed the small Manitoba town. He missed his memory of the town smelling like roses.

"You wake up in the morning and all you smell in your bedroom is the smell of roses," said Kyle to a *Winnipeg Free Press* reporter. The reporter wrote that Kyle still thought of Roseisle as a place where wild roses grew like weeds.

The last time he was in Roseisle, police had arrested him as he walked down the street and charged him with first-degree murder. Now he'd pay a fortune to go back one more time.

"I'd like to see [Roseisle] one last time on my terms to say goodbye," continued Kyle to the reporter. "How do you go to prison, enter in a nightmare, in a world that smells of roses?"

The time Kyle was locked up would be a part of his life he could neither forget nor avoid. He was not shy about his past. The idea of prison did not frighten him anymore. He'd spent almost all of his adult life in jail. He was there so long, it seemed more like a home compared to the real world.

A year after his release on bail, he threw a stone at a window with a police officer beside him so that he could be re-arrested and sent back to jail. His ploy did not work.

"My life doesn't belong to me, it belongs to the system still," Kyle said.

At the same time as Kyle was waiting to see if he got his freedom, former top Manitoba prosecutor George Dangerfield's cases were being questioned. Some of his most famous cases became miscarriages of justice. He was at the helm of two confirmed wrongful convictions — James Driskell and Thomas Sophonow. In both cases, judicial inquiries determined that Dangerfield committed errors and failed in his duty to disclose relevant evidence to the defence.

Dangerfield controlled the scale of justice, tipping it falsely in his favour. Now it was tipping the other way, and Kyle Unger might get his freedom. If that happened, Dangerfield would add another name to his list of the wrongfully convicted.

24

CHAPTER TWENTY-FOUR

TRUE FREEDOM

On October 10, 2009, Justice Minister Robert Nicholson was set to finally make an announcement concerning Kyle Unger. He had been out on bail for over four years, waiting for a decision. Whichever way it went, it would be life-changing for him.

On this morning, Robert Nicholson announced that Kyle's conviction had been overturned. A new trial would be ordered.

"I am satisfied there is a reasonable basis to conclude that a miscarriage of justice likely occurred in Mr. Unger's 1992 conviction," Nicholson said.

Kyle said he was not angry about what transpired.

"I'm pretty relieved," he said. "An opportunity to prove my innocence has finally come my way and I'm looking forward to it." He said he hadn't thought about potential compensation. The situation had dragged on and he wanted closure.

It was up to Manitoba Justice to determine whether to proceed with a new trial, have him formally acquitted, or stay the charges. The last option would allow the Crown to lay a murder charge at some point in the future if it believed it had new evidence. That had already happened to Kyle once. But they had already decided this was not an option after the James Driskell case. They found it left the accused with a permanent stigma in the community.

A retrial may have been a challenge to mount. The disproven hair was the only physical evidence linking Unger to the crime. The jailhouse informant testimony could not be used in court. The undercover sting that led to his confession had holes in it, because his recounting of the killing included several factual errors. The only witness who claimed to have seen Unger take part in Grenier's killing was Tim Houlahan. He had committed suicide in 1994 while awaiting a new trial. Overall, they wouldn't have much of a case against Kyle.

A hearing was held on October 23, 2009, to determine if there would be a retrial. Kyle's lawyer, Hersh Wolch, didn't present evidence for his defence. Instead, he went through discredited prosecution evidence against his client. He then told the judge and prosecutor that they should be ashamed of what happened to Kyle.

"It's not sufficient enough to say those were standards then," Wolch said. "You're wrong, and it had horrible consequences for this young man." He said prosecutors in the case were guilty of "one of the worst cases of tunnel vision ever committed. It has all the hallmarks of what causes a wrongful conviction."

Manitoba Justice Assistant Deputy Attorney General Don Slough represented the Crown. At first, Slough appeared to lay at least some of the blame for a wrongful conviction at Kyle's feet.

"Without Unger's willingness to confess to the horrific murder of a person he described as a friend, there was no case against him," said Slough, who'd worked with Crown Attorney George Dangerfield for over twenty years. "It had been suggested that the Crown's case against him is improbable and that his confession was inconsistent with the known facts. Those arguments were made to the jury and rejected."

Slough then went on to dismantle the Crown's case against Kyle. There was no DNA evidence linking Unger to the murder. The jailhouse informant could not be used in court. The Crown said the police did not disclose all the evidence in the case. Witnesses suggested that Tim Houlahan might have been a Satanist. In the original trial, they used Kyle's past brushes with the law against him, but they withheld information about Tim Houlahan's criminal past. They knew about a robbery Tim Houlahan had committed three years before the murder in which he broke into a woman's house, stole her underwear, and ripped up her marriage certificate.

The only evidence against Kyle was the confession and that was in question.

"Taking into account these circumstances, a group of very experienced Crown attorneys has reviewed the file," said Slough. "It is their conclusion that it would be unsafe to retry Unger on the available evidence.

"He is entitled to an acquittal. In the eyes of the law, he's an innocent man."

Associate Chief Justice Glenn Joyal told Unger he was directing an acquittal for Unger's first-degree murder conviction. He said he would face no further court action in the murder.

"There is nothing further I can say but good luck," Joyal said.

Kyle came out of the Winnipeg Law Courts building to be greeted by a sea of reporters. It was his first breath of fresh air as a free man. His acquittal was the first of its kind in Canada. Other wrongful convictions had resulted in a new trial or the charges being stayed, not acquitted.

Hersh Wolch said he felt the case was an example of improper procedures by RCMP and Crown prosecutors. "An innocent guy went to jail for a long time. We do have a historic day, but we haven't learned enough," said Wolch.

"It's the first day of the rest of my life," said Kyle to the reporters. "It's a new beginning . . . The hardest part [has been] waiting for it to come to an end. It's been a long journey, a long time in coming. It's surreal, almost."

Now that he was acquitted on a wrongful conviction, the question came down to compensation. Wrongfully convicted individuals usually received money for their loss. Compensation is not simply about money, but also about helping to remove the public stigma for someone wrongfully convicted of murder. David Milgaard received $10 million, James Driskell got $4 million, and Steven Truscott $6.5 million.

Two hours after Kyle was acquitted, Manitoba Attorney General Dave Chomiak said the province would not pay a dime in compensation to Unger for the fourteen years spent in prison. They argued that a jury convicted Unger of the Grenier slaying largely based on his confession to undercover police officers.

"The sad reality of the entire tragedy is that had it not been told to an undercover police officer that he killed

Brigitte Grenier, even all the other available evidence would not have sent him to jail," Chomiak said. "Without his confession, he would not have been charged. Without his confession, he would not have been convicted. Twelve men and women in a jury convicted him."

Chomiak said Unger was not entitled to compensation because he was not proven innocent of the crime; he was only found not guilty because no evidence was called.

Along with the compensation announcement, Chomiak also said he would not call a public inquiry into Unger's Crown prosecution. A Manitoba RCMP spokesperson said there were no plans to reopen the investigation into Grenier's case.

Kyle was happy to be acquitted and not immediately focused on compensation.

"I spent twenty years wanting my life back. I got it back today, and I'm trying to absorb the fact that I got what was most important to me — my freedom, my exoneration, my innocence proven," Kyle said. "It's going to take some time to really figure it out."

Currently, the only financial remedy for the wrongfully convicted — unless found factually innocent — is to launch a claim for malicious prosecution, negligent investigation, prosecutorial misconduct, false imprisonment, or perhaps a claim for breach under the Charter of Rights and Freedoms.

On September 21, 2011, Kyle Unger filed a $14.5 million wrongful conviction lawsuit. In the statement of claim filed in the Manitoba Court of Queen's Bench, he named as defendants the RCMP, individual RCMP members, and specific Crown attorneys, as well as both the federal and provincial Attorney Generals.

"The grievous loss, damage, and expense sustained by the plaintiff included loss of freedom, loss of enjoyment of life, severe emotional trauma and distress. He was deprived of his youth, his education, and a normal working life," read the statement of claims.

Unger's claim gathered dust without a response from any of the defendants for nearly two years. In August 2013, that changed when the federal justice minister filed a firm denial of Unger's allegations. Kyle continued to look for compensation from the government. His post-jail life continued in British Columbia near his parents. He worked on various construction crews. He still waits for the payment he thinks he deserves. He might have won his freedom, but this last fight might not go his way.

★ ★ ★

On the night of June 23, 1990, teenage friends Kyle Unger and John Beckett made a last-minute decision to attend the Woodstick Music Festival. They were considered to be loners, not the popular kids at school. But, on this night, they seemed to finally fit in. They had fun, played games, drank, and hung around the bonfire with other people. By the next morning, a sixteen-year-old girl was dead. By the next week, Kyle was charged with her murder. For the next twenty years, he fought for his freedom. He fought to survive many years in jail. He fought to regain his place in the world. Now came his biggest struggle — to live a normal life. This may be the hardest thing for him to do, because normal doesn't come easy to a person who has gone through so much. Maybe one day, he will get to go back to Roseisle and wake up to the smell of roses.

AFTERWORD

The criminal justice system exists to convict and punish the guilty. But convicting the innocent creates two failures: someone is unjustly punished and a criminal goes free. Wrongful convictions do involve a third tragic dimension. The family of the victim is left twisting in the wind, not able to accept that the person they have grown to hate may be innocent. They are often unable to undo the passionate feelings that may have been built up against that person.

Over the years, the Greniers struggled. Mariette Grenier, Brigitte's older sister by one and a half years, moved away from home three months after the murder happened.

"There were too many memories in the house," she said. Her parents tried to hold onto the memory of their youngest daughter. They wanted to remember the good things: her smile, her heart of gold, the special times together.

The Grenier family has maintained that they believe in Kyle Unger's guilt.

"When they say it was the most brutal murder, it was," said one Grenier family member. "You can guess how I feel about whoever did this to her."

When the case was opened up for review, they were deeply disappointed. No matter what evidence was disproved, they still believed Kyle was guilty.

"I am sure there is no doubt about it," said Ron Grenier, Brigitte's father. "Welcome to Canada's greatest justice system — free all murderers across the country . . . My family has been demolished, starting nineteen years ago, and it hasn't ended. The system just plainly doesn't work and it always favours the person who committed the crime."

As it stands, no one is being held responsible for Brigitte Grenier's slaying. There is reason to believe that no one will ever be held accountable. The last victim in this case is the original one, Brigitte Grenier.

EPILOGUE:
NEW RULES FOR THE MR. BIG STING

The Mr. Big sting police operation was developed in Canada by the RCMP in the 1990s to help solve cold cases. The controversial police tactic has been used more than 350 times with a 95 per cent rate of conviction. But it has not always been successful. Some confessions obtained through these stings have turned out to be false. People have been wrongfully convicted because of it.

On July 31, 2014, the Supreme Court of Canada decided to crack down on Mr. Big stings. The Supreme Court makes decisions to properly convict the guilty and protect the innocent. They look for ways to prevent wrongful convictions. The Court wanted the Mr. Big procedure to be carefully examined before being admissible in court. The top court did not ban the tactic. Instead, they introduced a tough new standard for trial judges to consider. This included the reliability of the confession, as well as police conduct during the investigation.

"The Mr. Big technique comes at a price," wrote Supreme Court Justice Michael Moldaver about their decision. He continued to state that the operation could be abusive and produce unreliable confessions. However, he also noted that the sting can produce valuable evidence.

The court ruled that rather than being routinely allowed, the Crown must prove at trial that the confessions meet a two-stage test. First, the confession must be proven to be reliable; and second, the judge must examine the police conduct during the investigation.

The Supreme Court's decision sent a message for future Mr. Big operations. The state strongly encourages that police officers be more careful in how they conduct their operations. Mr. Big stings are still allowed, however the police must walk a fine line between encouraging a confession and bribing or coercing the target into giving a confession. In the end, the judge will have to decide whether the police have gained a valuable piece of evidence, or prompted a false confession.

TIMELINE

JUNE 23, 1990: Woodstick Music Festival occurs near Roseisle, Manitoba.

JUNE 24, 1990: Two cyclists find Brigitte Grenier's nude body near the festival site, submerged in a creek. The freckle-faced Miami Collegiate class president had been strangled, battered on the head, bitten, and impaled with sticks. Police call it one of the most horrifying murders in Manitoba's history.

JUNE 29, 1990: Kyle Unger and Timothy Houlahan, who did not know each other, are charged with first-degree murder.

DECEMBER 11, 1990: During a preliminary inquiry, charges against Unger are stayed.

JUNE 1991: Police charge Unger with murder again after he confesses to undercover RCMP officers in a Mr. Big sting.

JANUARY 20, 1992: Trial for both men begins. Houlahan stands trial as an adult.

FEBRUARY 28, 1992: Unger, now 21, and Houlahan, 19, convicted of first-degree murder, sentenced to life in jail with no chance of parole for 25 years.

JULY 7, 1993: Unger's appeal is dismissed. Manitoba Court of Appeal orders a new trial for Houlahan but he commits suicide in 1994 before a trial is held.

APRIL 23, 2003: Prompted by several high-profile allegations of wrongful convictions, the province of Manitoba sets up a committee to review all murder convictions involving hair analysis as key evidence.

JULY 27, 2004: DNA evidence challenges evidence that linked Unger to Grenier's murder.

SEPTEMBER 13, 2004: Unger files an application with the Attorney General of Canada for a ministerial review of his conviction.

NOVEMBER 5, 2005: Unger is released on bail.

MARCH 11, 2009: Ottawa concludes Unger was likely the victim of a miscarriage of justice and orders Manitoba to conduct a new trial.

OCTOBER 23, 2009: Unger walks out of court a free man. No evidence is presented against him at his new trial and he is acquitted.

SEPTEMBER 22, 2011: Unger files a $14.5 million lawsuit for his wrongful conviction.

JULY 31, 2014: The Supreme Court of Canada releases tough new standards for trial judges who are hearing cases that involve the use of Mr. Big police operations.

GLOSSARY

ACQUITTAL: the verdict when someone accused of a crime is found not guilty.

APPEAL: a request to review a case that has already been decided in court.

CHARGE TO THE JURY: when a judge instructs the jury about what law(s) to apply to the case and how to carry out its duties in deciding the verdict.

CONVICTION: the verdict when someone accused of a crime is found guilty.

CROSS-EXAMINATION: after a witness for either the defence or for the Crown tells what he or she knows, a lawyer for the other side gets to ask questions of the witness.

CROWN ATTORNEY: the lawyer(s) acting for the government, or "the Crown," in court proceedings. They are the prosecutors in Canada's legal system.

DEFENDANT: the person who has been formally accused of and charged with committing a crime.

FORENSICS: the study of medical facts in relation to legal cases.

FIRST-DEGREE MURDER: the planned or deliberate killing of another human being. In Canada, there are thirteen conditions under which someone can be charged with first-degree murder. Murder while committing or attempting to commit aggravated sexual assault is one of them.

JURY: a criminal trial is decided by a group of twelve randomly selected citizens from the province in which the trial is held. All twelve must agree on a verdict.

MR. BIG STING: a police tactic in which a number of undercover police officers pose as a criminal organization and target someone they believe is guilty of a serious crime. They pretend to recruit the person into their group, often promising money and other incentives in return for a confession to the serious crime.

PRELIMINARY HEARING: a hearing held to decide if there is enough evidence for a trial. This is held after the accused has been charged with a crime.

PROSECUTOR: the lawyer acting for the prosecution usually the state (in Canada, the Crown). The prosecutor tries to prove the defendant is guilty.

TESTIMONY: the statement of a witness under oath.

TRANSCRIPTS: word-for-word written reports of a trial.

VERDICT: the decision of the jury at the end of a trial, usually guilty or not guilty.

FURTHER READING

ONLINE:

The Fifth Estate, "The Wrong Man," at www.cbc.ca/fifth/
episodes/2009-2010/the-wrong-man.

ONLINE RADIO:

"Freeing the Innocent: 20 years of AIDWYC," at www.
cbc.ca/thesundayedition/features/2013/10/27/
feature-8/.

ONLINE ARTICLES:

Bruce A. Macfarlane, "Wrongful Convictions: Is it
Proper for the Crown to Root Around, Looking for
Miscarriages of Justice?" *Manitoba Law Journal*, Vol.
36, Issue 1 at http://robsonhall.ca/mlj/sites/default/
files/articles/MacFarlane%20-%20Wrongful%20
Convictions.pdf.

The Forensic Evidence Review Committee Final
Report at www.gov.mb.ca/justice/publications/for-
ensic/finalreport_forensic2004.pdf.

The 1993 Court of Appeal decision for Kyle Unger: *R.
v. Unger*, 1993 CanLII 4409 (MB CA) at http://canlii.
ca/t/1pfk2.

The 2005 application for the ministerial review of Kyle Unger's conviction: *R. v. Unger*, 2005 MBQB 238 (CanLII) at http://canlii.ca/t/1lzgl.

The 2005 conditions of Kyle Unger's release: *R. v. Unger*, 2005 MBQB 242 (CanLII) at http://canlii. ca/t/1m0tv.

The 2014 Supreme Court decision relating to Mr. Big operations by police at http://scc-csc.lexum.com/ scc-csc/scc-csc/en/item/14031/index.do.

ACKNOWLEDGEMENTS

In preparing this book, I tried to use as many primary sources as possible. This includes original transcripts of the preliminary hearings, the trial, the various appeals, and Supreme Court hearings. I would like to thank the people at the Queens Court Bench at the Manitoba Law Courts Building in Winnipeg. They provided me access to this primary source material.

My other source of information to tell the story of Kyle Unger came from the *Winnipeg Free Press* and *Winnipeg Sun* newspapers. Over the past twenty-four years their reporters have covered this case in-depth. This includes the investigations, trials, and events leading up to Unger's acquittal. These journalists helped paint a picture of the case as it evolved and the feelings surrounding these events. For the *Winnipeg Free Press* this included journalists Gabrielle Giroday, Dan Lett, Nick Martin, Bruce Owen, Aldo Santin, Mike McIntyre, James Turner, Paul Wiecek, Kevin Rollason, and Maureen Houston. For the *Winnipeg Sun* this included journalists Dawna Dingwall, Judy Owen, Donna Carreiro, Jeffrey Slusky, and James O'Connor.

I am also thankful for the continued support of James Lorimer & Company and the guidance of my editor, Pam Hickman.

INDEX